Which Life to Live

A Novel by Robert English

Dedication

This book is dedicated to what started as two challenges, became two critics, and are now my best friends - BRGE and CJEE.

Prologue

"Enter by the narrow gate. For the gate is wide and the way is easy that leads to destruction, and those who enter by it are many." Matthew 7:1

Myth: a traditional or legendary story, usually concerning some being or hero or event, with or without a determinable basis of fact or natural explanation.

Ministry: a profession, duties; the act of serving

Kristine Locke, a beautiful, talented young lady and Mark Hiott a handsome bright young man were faced with the same three choices as each planned their life.

Will it be the life they want to live?
Will it be the life they could live?
Will it be the life they should live?

Kristine Locke slid into a life she wanted realizing that it would not only tear her away from high school sweetheart Hiott, but also present an exciting world of myths and legends. What she wasn't expecting was a myth becoming a reality and pushing her into a life of deceit and fear.

Mark Hiott chose a life that he wanted, could and should live. The Ministry was his calling, a calling where he found success, satisfaction, and comfort.

It was more than fate that brought Kristine back to Mark and totally devastating when she was accidentally ripped her away from Mark again. What Kristine left behind was a secret life that was a mystery to Mark, a mystery that Mark needed answers to.

Chapter 1

It was one of those typical Southern Ontario mid March evenings in 1988. The wind off the lake picked up and was blowing a cool dampness across Hamilton Bay. The worst of winter may have passed, but the temperature still hovered near the freezing point all day, and as night approached, a rain-snow mix began filtering down from the overcast sky. The downtown parking lots were now empty and only a few people hustled briskly on the wet sidewalks.

Reverend Mark Hiott and his wife Kristine made reservations at their favourite restaurant in downtown Hamilton to celebrate Mark's thirty-eighth birthday in style. The Italian Bistro was a relatively short drive from their house and the only stop they made was for a red light at the corner where the same panhandler ran his business for a few years. The panhandler recognized Mark's car and immediately approached. Mark rolled the window down as he did each time he passed by and tossed some loose change into the man's paper cup and was repaid with a toothless smile and a thank you.

As soon as they walked through the restaurant door, the aroma of garlic and oregano flooded their senses. The owner, a short older man, greeted them with a firm handshake and a wide grin.

"Ciao, it's so good to see you again. Let me take your coats and I'll show you to your table."

Kristine answered for both of them. "Thank you."

A corner table in the dimly lit restaurant was a perfect setting for the celebration. Both ordered a small glass of red wine and clinked glasses as Kristine wished him a happy birthday. She passed him an envelope that he quickly opened. Inside were a birthday card and a gift certificate from his book store.

"Kristine, this is perfect. Thank you Dear."

The dinner was much more than either usually ate in the evening. Bread, salad, pasta, dessert and coffee spanned an hour and a half.

Over a second coffee, their discussion was something that became more important in recent weeks. After a battery of medical testing, it turned out that Kristine was not able to have children. He knew that she was deeply disappointed and cried when the doctor told her.

"Kristine, this might be a good time to talk about the elephant in the room."

"Oh Mark, I so wanted a family. I feel like I disappointed you."

"We're in this together and we need to find a solution together." Mark paused and sipped his coffee. In a low voice, he asked, "Should we consider adoption?"

"I don't know. That is a big step but it seems to be our only option."

Mark smiled, reached over and took Kristine's hand. "Yes it is. Let's think about it a bit more."

Kristine squeezed his hand. No, I don't need any time Mark. Let's start the adoption process."

"I agree." Mark was elated as his Christian values saw family as one of the most important things that any man could have. Kristine always wanted children and was now so very happy that they agreed to bring a child into their lives. No evening could have been any better than this. He stared into her deep green eyes, leaned across the table and kissed her.

They left the restaurant full and happy walking hand and hand to the car that was now covered with slushy snow. Mark brushed it off as the vehicle warmed up and Kristine tuned in a station that was playing soft instrumentals. As soon as the car pulled away from the lot, they did what they always did after leaving this particular restaurant; reflect on the homemade pasta that was covered with Nona Maria's famous tomato sauce. It was a sauce straight from Northern Italy and lingered on one's lips for a couple of days after it was eaten. Mark enjoyed cooking as his hobby, but he never was able to duplicate the taste.

They lived in Hamilton for two years and it was still a challenge for Mark to find his way around easily, especially downtown. On the way home, traffic was light as they began to weave through the city's one way streets. The wet snow was not accumulating but the roads were a bit slick.

Kristine couldn't resist having a bit of fun. "Mark, maybe we should adopt an Italian baby, that way you have to make spaghetti every day."

"I have enough trouble keeping the pounds off now between your cooking and the sweet treats when I visit my congregation." Mark quipped. "Besides, you're a steak gal."

Kristine reached over and put her hand behind his head and lightly stroked the nape of his neck. "This steak gal loves a Minister."

****

Mark did not see the delivery truck coming from the street to his right. It sped through the red light slamming into Mark's car with full impact on the passenger's door. The crash was deafening. Thousands of pieces of glass flew through the car and Mark's head bounced violently off the driver's side window with tremendous impact. The repercussion sent a sharp pain through his neck and his lap belt dug into both sides of his lower torso. The car was pushed sideways across the pavement until the curb stopped it from banging into a building. Mark slowly opened his eyes trying to get oriented. He could feel a warm liquid running down the left side of his face. His neck throbbed and there was a severe jabbing in his left leg. He could hear the sound of sirens off in the distance as he slowly turned his head trying to focus on Kristine. She wasn't moving. Broken glass and blood covered her face and she sat lifeless, her head slumped over with only the seat belt holding her body in place. He reached over and shook her shoulder and yelled her name, but there was no reaction. He did it again; still no reaction. He could smell fuel and could see the damaged front of a large truck pushed up against his car. Flames from under the truck were getting higher and he could feel the heat. Mark heard people yelling and he felt hands pulling him from the car just before he passed out.

Mark awoke to a lot of pain. Slowly opening his eyes, he could see a white ceiling with a large square light above him. A beeping sound cut through the silence every few seconds. He tried to shift his head from side to side, but a neck brace prevented any movement. Confused, with a throbbing head, he reached up painfully with his right hand and felt a large bandage wrapped all the way around his head. He lowered his eyes and saw his left leg in a plastic cast slightly elevated on the bed. Still dazed and under sedation, he became aware that there was someone coming into the room. A nurse proceeded to the side of his bed to change his intravenous bag and check the tape on his arm. Everything was so foggy and his mind slowly returned to the accident; the sounds, the smells, and the sights, especially Kristine sitting motionless covered in blood and not responding. Oh, my God, he thought as tears began to fill his eyes.

Words interrupted his thoughts.

"Reverend Hiott, I'm Dr. Hanna. It's good that you are awake. I'd like to have a quick look at you. Do you remember what happened?"

"I know we were in an accident. How is my wife, Kristine?"

"Reverend Hiott, I have some very bad news for you. Kristine didn't make it."

"She's dead," Mark gasped?

"Yes, she died at the scene. There was nothing that the paramedics could do."

"How did she die?"

"She suffered a severe chest compression and a major head injury. It would have been quick."

Mark lay in the bed with his eyes closed and saying a silent prayer for his wife.

"Doctor, how long have I been unconscious?"

"Twelve hours. You took quite a hit to your head. I believe it was from banging it against the window. There are a few stitches in your scalp, but our tests revealed no severe head trauma. A small stress fracture to your left leg will require a walking cast for a week or so."

"What about my neck?"

"The brace is only precautionary and should come off soon. The x rays were negative. Listen Reverend Hiott, I do not mean to be insensitive. Losing your wife is terrible, but a lot of people are depending on you and you need to focus on recovery. You'll be here for at least another day to make sure that you don't have any lingering effects of the concussion and your other injuries are healing. I'll be back in a few hours to check up. In the meantime, if there is anything you need, just press the button for the nurse." With that, the doctor left the room.

Mark closed his eyes but couldn't stop the tears rolling down his cheeks. He was trying to comprehend what this really meant. His wife was gone. A terrible feeling of loneliness invaded his entire being. A familiar voice broke the silence.

"Mark, can you hear me? It's Jim Andrews."

"Yes Jim."

"How are you feeling Mark?"

"Devastated. I lost Kristine."

'Mark, I am so sorry."

After a long silence, Jim Andrews spoke. "A policeman has been waiting for you to regain consciousness. They have a few questions. Do you feel up to speaking with him?"

"Jim, give me a few minutes and send him in."

Mark lay there replaying the final few minutes he had with Kristine. He could still feel her hand on the back of his neck and repeated her final words, 'This steak gal loves a Minister. This steak gal loves a Minister'.

A voice brought Mark back to the moment and he could see a tall uniformed woman standing beside his bed. "Reverend Hiott, I'm Officer Singh. Are you up to answering a few questions?"

"Yes."

"My condolences in losing your wife."

"Thank you."

"Sir, so you remember the accident?"

"I recall seeing bright lights coming towards the passenger side of the car and a huge crash. My head hit the window and when I turned toward Kristine, I could see a large truck hit us. I remember calling her but she didn't respond. The next thing I wake up here. What happened?"

"An eye witness confirmed that the truck went through a red light. The roads were slick but that really didn't contribute to the accident. The driver of the truck was impaired and died a few hours after the accident from injuries. He wasn't wearing a seat belt. We were able to find out that he was coming off a late night delivery to a storage place downtown. Apparently, he stopped for a few beers after his work. Your car is a write-off."

"My car is a write-off? That is the very least of my concerns."

The policeman could see Mark's eyes welling up.

"Reverend, I have only one more question. Did you have anything to drink before the accident?"

"I had a six ounce glass of wine at dinner about two hours before the accident."

"Thank you Sir. I think I have all I need. Again my condolences."

Jim Andrews came back into the room.

"Jim, where is Kristine?"

"She is at the Coroner's office waiting for direction."

"Can I ask you to do me a favour?'

"Anything Mark."

"Can you arrange for her to be sent to Clarrington's Funeral Home?" Tell them that as soon as I get out, I'll come by and finalize arrangements."

"I'll take care of it as soon as I leave here. Mark, as you would think, there was very wide media coverage about the accident. The Church has been flooded with calls from your parishioners and they were told to avoid visiting until advised. Now that we know you are okay, I'll make sure that they know your status. In the meantime, don't worry about your congregation. Presbytery is aware and has options to hold the fort while you recover. I'll leave you to rest and come back tomorrow. Oh, I should tell you that I called your father. I thought they should know before they read or heard about it. Kristine's mother, your parents and sister and brother-in-law are arriving this evening. No doubt, they will want to see you."

"Thanks Jim."

"Is there anything I can do Mark?"

"I need some time Jim."

Chapter 2

Kristine's and Mark's families arrived from Regina just after dinner. They invaded his room full of anxiety with Mark's mother the first to his bedside. After a few minutes of tears and kisses, Mark reached out for Kristine's mother and pulled her closer.

"I'm so sorry,' he said.

"Mark it wasn't your fault. She loved you and even though she left us too early, Kristine lived a full life."

Realizing the sombre mood in the room and reaching into his ministerial training, Mark took the lead.

"Mrs. Locke, I am not sure you know this but Kristine and I agreed that if something should happen to either one of us, we would prefer cremation after the service."

"Mark, I fully understand."

"I made arrangements for Kristine to go to Clarrington's Funeral Home."

"Is there anything we can do?" Mark's mother asked

"No. I need to take care of this myself."

"We understand," Mark's father said before changing the subject. "Did the doctor give you any idea how long you will be here?"

"He's coming by later. I hope that I can be released tomorrow.

The following late morning, his father and brother in law Russ were on hand to help him home. Thinking ahead, Russ rented a van to not only transport the families in Hamilton but also to make it easier on Mark's leg.

As Mark hobbled into the house on his crutches, the families were silent knowing that this would be a very emotional moment. It would be the first time that there would be no Kristine waiting.

Mark remained composed. "I want to thank all of you for being here. There still is so much to do but first I want to go to the funeral home. Mrs. Locke, I know you want to go as well. Does anyone else want to go" he asked giving off a vibe that he hoped they wouldn't.

Mark's father looked around and responded for them all. "No, you go ahead. Russ, can you drive them and wait?"

"Yes."

"Thanks Russ," Mark said.

Within a few minutes Mrs. Locke and Mark were being chauffeured to the funeral home. Russ helped Mark inside then returned to the van to wait.

Larry Clarrington was waiting in the entry way.

"Reverend Hiott my sincere condolences."

"Thank you Larry. This is Kristine's mother, Mrs. Locke."

"Mrs. Locke, I am sorry for your loss."

"Thank you Mr. Clarrington."

"Larry, can we see Kristine?"

"By all means. This way please. Let me give you some time. I'll be in my office when you finish."

Mrs. Locke was first to approach the open casket and spent quite a few minutes quietly weeping and stroking Kristine's hair. She backed away slowly and hugged Mark before sitting on a nearby chair.

Mark had prepared many families for what was about to happen but he never realized the overwhelming grief that was about to come over him. He couldn't control his emotions and stayed leaning over the casket for several minutes with his head resting on Kristine's hands that were draped across her chest. He kissed her forehead gently then wiped the tears away and stepped back, taking Mrs. Locke's arm and silently leading her toward the office.

"Please have a seat. Once again, my condolences to both you Mrs. Locke and to you Reverend Hiott."

"Thank you Larry."

"Have you given any thought to arrangements?"

"Yes. I would like three visitations then a Church service in three days. Kristine will be cremated and a private interment at a later date. Mrs. Locke, do you agree?"

"Yes, Mark."

****

Back at Mark's house during a quiet lunch that his mother and sister prepared, Mark found out that the family checked in at a local hotel and immediately reacted.

"I'm so sorry, I never thought. I have lots of room here. Please stay."

Mark's mother answered. "Mark, do you have three spare bedrooms?"

"Yes. In fact, we have four as well as three bathrooms. Remember, these old manses were built for large families. Kristine made sure that we were always prepared for visitors. Besides, I would appreciate the company."

"I would like that Mark," Mrs. Locke replied

"Okay son," said Marks' father.

Mark's mother asked, "Mark, how are you feeling? You were unconscious for a few hours and you have cuts and bruises."

"Thank goodness for medicine. The doctor gave me pills and they are working well."

The room stayed quiet for quite a few minutes. Still sitting around the dining table, Mark addressed a subject that everyone was thinking but no one wanted to talk about.

"I have been giving some thought to Kristine's final resting place and I would like her to be in Regina. You know she is being cremated and once I fully recover, I would like to bring her to Regina and conduct an interment service."

"Why Regina?" Mark's father asked.

"Dad, I know that my career could take me anywhere. If Kristine is interred in Hamilton, she may wind up alone. At least this way, there will be family and friends. In addition, I have decided to add to my will interment in Regina. There is something you can do for me. Can you find a plot for us? I'll pay."

"Yes Son, I will take care of that."

"There are a few other things that need to be done. This afternoon I need to get an obituary to the paper and talk to Reverend Jim Andrews regarding the service and the Church ladies for the reception. I was hoping that you Mrs. Locke, Mom and Sis, could take care of ordering flowers and pick some appropriate photos for the memory board. Russ, I'll need to do a bit of running around. Could you continue chauffeuring?"

"No problem Mark."

Chapter 3

The visitations were a steady stream of people and by the end of the second evening. Mark was exhausted. Between the lingering pain, the medications and the walking cast, he decided to forego the last visitation and prepare himself for the funeral that included some last minute prayers and hymns for Jim Andrews to include.

The pews were full by 10:15 for the 11:00 a.m. service. A large crowd was anticipated and the service would be piped into a large meeting room that held an additional forty attendees. In the sanctuary many of Hamilton's Clergy from various denominations and city officials that knew Mark sat among the crowd. A couple of Kristine's sorority sisters who lived in Hamilton came as well. Mark sat on the aisle in the front row. Beside him was Mrs. Locke, then his parents followed by Janet and Russ. Kristine's casket in was no more than ten feet in front of Mark. Several large floral arrangements were on stands throughout the altar and a large spray of red roses that Mark's sister arranged for was draped over the casket. Soft organ music played in the background until Jim Andrews entered from the side, the cue for people to rise.

The service proceeded as laid out in the Order of Service with most people waiting anxiously for Mark to deliver the eulogy. As he rose, Andrews came down from the pulpit to assist Mark to the lectern. Now standing facing a full sanctuary, he tried desperately to retain his composure remembering that he comforted many families who lost loved ones and a funeral service was really a celebration of life. Mark spoke elegantly and lovingly with a few humorous inserts but mostly about Kristine's life, both before they married and after. He included the innocent way they met at high school, going separate ways, then reuniting happily. He stressed how she enjoyed being a Minister's wife and how so many people complimented her on her Church and community activities. He kept his words to eight minutes knowing that was as long as his composure would hold out. As he returned to his seat, he noticed that there were very few dry eyes in the congregation.

For the remainder of the service, Mark sat feeling the emotional pain, a strong sense of loneliness, fear, and an inner numbness. He kept asking questions of his God. Each time he reached deeper and remembered what he told so many others who grieved; faith and scripture would heal him over time.

Mark, Mrs. Locke and his family followed the casket out the door to the waiting hearse. As the vehicle door closed, Mark could feel his family's hands on his shoulders as he held Mrs. Locke's hand.

Mark reached forward and touched the casket. "Good bye Kristine. May God be with you my love."

As usual, the ladies prepared a large buffet luncheon that followed the service. The lower hall was full as the crowd shuffled by the food tables then around the walls to look at pictures that Mark's sister put together.

By the time 2:00 came, only a few people remained. Mark thanked the women and the family went back to Mark's house and sat at the dining room table drinking coffee and tea.

****

The following day was consumed by family conversation and reminiscing. At dinner, Janet asked, "Mark, is there anything else we can do?" Maybe I should stay for a while?"

"No Sis, you have done so much already. Thank you."

As coffee was being poured, Mark spoke. "Dad, Russ, can I speak with you in the parlour?"

When the three men were alone, Mark's father spoke. "What is it son?"

"There are two things. I need to change my will. Kristine was the beneficiary so I would like to change to half going to Presbyterian World Service and half to Janet and you, Russ."

"Mark, why Janet and me?"

"Russ, I am a realist and know that the likelihood of meeting someone else is remote. Russ, you and Janet have four children and they will need money for an education. Can you rework my will?"

"Yes, I can do that and there is always time to make more changes down the road."

"You said two things Mark."

"Yes Dad. This afternoon I received a letter couriered from the lawyer for the company that the truck driver worked for and they have already made me an out of court settlement. I need advice."

"Well Mark, the attempt to get a quick settlement is not uncommon, but this much speedier than I have ever heard. I am suspicious and I know that any offer is usually less than what a court would award. Can you give me the letter? I will act as your legal representative, pro bono of course. Let me rattle them."

"Dad, I don't want this to get messy.'

"I hear you Mark."

****

Two days after the funeral, the family left to return to Regina. They hadn't been gone more than an hour when there was a knock on the door. It was Larry Clarrington

"Good afternoon Rev. Hiott. You asked me to bring Kristine's ashes to you."

"Yes Larry. I appreciate this. By way, your staff did an excellent job. The family and I want to thank you."

"I'll pass along your gratitude."

"Did you bring along your invoice?"

"No. We usually mail them out two weeks after the service."

"I'll watch for it and drop a cheque off."

As soon as Clarrington left, Mark put the urn on the mantle beside their wedding picture knowing that she would be in her final resting place soon.

Later that day, Mark retrieved Kristine's will from a documents box that they kept in the bedroom closet. He opened it up and read through it. It contained standard statements. There was a short list of bequests mostly some personal items like a watch she bought after university going to her mother. Also, she asked that one thousand of a ten thousand dollar life insurance policy be given to a local shelter for the homeless. As Mark was putting the will back in the manila holder it was blocked by something. He reached inside and pulled out a small white envelope. It was sealed with no writing on it. Before he had a chance to open it, the telephone rang and Mark dropped the envelope back in the holder. The call was from a parishioner having difficulty with his daughter and was looking for advice. The call went on for almost an hour and after he hung up, he felt badly for the parishioner, but felt good sensing he was getting back to his role as a Minister. Back in the bedroom, he put the folder back in the document box and returned the box to the closet.

Following doctor's orders, two weeks passed at home and Mark was bored. His neck brace was gone, the deep forehead cut was healing nicely and a walking cast was off but still had a slight limp. The time was filled with addressing Kristine's bequests, paying for the funeral related expenses and completing countless forms for his insurance company. The money for the car came quickly and he decided that once his foot was fully recovered, he would pay a visit to the car dealer in his congregation. It was now time to concentrate on his first sermon back. Would it be on grief, or on remorse, or on eternal life? His mind went back to his university mentor, Reverend Paul Morris. How would he approach this? No doubt, it would be a positive message.

A few days before Mark's planned return to the pulpit, his father called late in the afternoon.

"Hi Mark. How are you doing son?"

"As well as to be expected Dad. The headaches have been gone for a few days, the cut is healed and I am walking without a cast or cane. In fact, I just got in after buying a new car."

"Mark, how are you, really?"

"I'm still hurting Dad but time will heal me and my faith is secure."

"That's good to hear. Listen, I purchased a plot and will mail you the deed. It's in Hilltop Cemetery and near a large maple tree. When do you think you'll be coming with Kristine?"

"Not sure yet. I need to get back to the congregation. Perhaps late summer."

"Russ has a draft of your revised will. I'll send it along with the deed. Get back to him with ant corrections or changes. It will take a few weeks or even months to finalize."

"Thanks Dad."

"There is one other thing. It's about the settlement."

"Any progress?"

"Yes. The initial offer was $100,000."

Mark almost dropped the phone. "$100,000, did you say $100,000?"

"Yes."

"That's and awful lot of money. What do we do?"

"Nothing now. They agreed to a counter offer that I made. It wasn't easy, but all you need to do is sign off."

"You counter offered?"

"Yes, and after a few telephone calls and letters, I have agreement for $175,000."

"$175,000. Did I hear you correctly? Dad what is this all about?"

"The truck driver didn't stop for a few drinks. The police investigation uncovered the truth within a day of the accident. It turns out that there was a retirement party at his office and he got into the drink quite heavily. Several people admitted to telling him not to take the truck. They even told the Manager that he was drunk but nothing was done. The company is a subsidiary of a major national firm. Their liability is extensive and they are concerned that a public court case would impact their business."

"$175,000?"

"Yes Mark, $175,000."

"Dad, I never..."

"Mark, no one can put a value on human life and to you, Kristine was priceless, but I think that she would be happy to know that your life is now secure."

Chapter 4

Mark learned as a Minister that grief can manifest itself in many ways. Often it was a trip down memory lane for those in pain and it was no different for Mark. His thoughts continued to return to the past, back to the times he enjoyed with Kristine, his youth and even his childhood.

Mark was a typical little boy in the 1950's growing up in Regina. Everything was an adventure especially grade school. Playing outside with his friends was the most important part of the day and he seldom got into trouble. Like most families in the post war era, Sunday morning was more often than not reserved for Sunday school. Mark didn't get a lot out of those classes but as he moved into the ministry he realized that those times provided the foundation for his beliefs. His older sister, Janet, was cute and popular with her girlfriends as well as the boys and their mother kept a keen eye on her making sure that she was well aware that one moment of love can turn into a lifetime of indifference. That lifetime of indifference hit close to home. Their aunt paid the price for a wild lifestyle, got pregnant at sixteen, was hastily married, abandoned with a one year old, and wound up working two jobs in Calgary to avoid going on welfare. Mark's mother and father remained as supportive as possible of the aunt and Mark's cousin for several years until she died of pneumonia and the boy disappeared. Mark was often the fly on the wall when his mother was giving Janet the 'no sex' lecture again. He laughed knowing that Janet was bright and would not jeopardize a good future for one night of romance. The boys in the neighbourhood knew this all too well.

Mark enjoyed intra-mural sports but didn't have the inherent skill or drive to be good athletically. His grade school marks were excellent and teachers always reported good things during the parent-teacher interviews. He was very articulate and thoughtful of others, and most importantly, not easily led. By the end of grade school he became known for his laid back nature taking the time to absorb and process fully. His parents knew he was more than just cautious; he was very bright and slotted for the academic stream in high school.

Mark soon learned that high school was divided into groups. There were the jocks, both male and female, the group destined for a trade, and the last group that was deemed more likely to be going on to a higher education and good careers. The groups formed quickly as the first term in grade nine ended and with Mark's grades in the high 80's, he quickly became a favourite of the teachers. There was never any problem getting assignments done and handed in on time. By the start of grade ten, Mark was asked to participate in a mentoring program where some of the other students needing a bit of help could call on him to improve their marks. Mark was perfect for the role. He loved helping people, enjoyed spending time with fellow students and making new friends. One of those he liked to help was Kristine Locke. Kristine was doing well with English and History, but Math was giving her some difficulty.

Kristine wasn't what most would call beautiful but was marginally attractive. She was average height and a bit on the thin side. Her strongest asset was her personality. It was a combination of her smile, looking people in the eye when she spoke to others and oozing empathy. Her dark auburn hair and deep green eyes were her best features at that time. Since their first meeting in September 1965, they got along very well, enjoying each other's company at least once a week after school. They knew it was a friend to friend type of arrangement but high schoolers often read relationships differently and saw their friendship much more serious than Mark and Kristine experienced. By the end of the year, Kristine's Math grades improved to a B minus.

Throughout the next couple of years, Mark and Kristine became closer and by the end of grade eleven, both began to develop mature bodies and adult looks. They reserved the week days for school and personal activities and for Mark it was swimming and for Kristine it was volleyball. At the same time, their relationship was beginning to become more serious. Mark remembered the day very well. It was a Thursday after school at Kristine's house. They had just finished reviewing integers and roots. Mark collected his books and was about to open the front door when Kristine put her hand on his arm and asked if he wanted to go to a movie on Saturday night and she would treat. Mark picked Kristine up at 6:30 for the 7:20 showing of Thunderball. A lot of the students from the school were there, most in the back rows. Mark and Kristine sat in the middle, ten rows from the front. After the show, they went to the local hangout for fries and gravy. Mark paid at the restaurant as a way of making the evening a Dutch treat.

The relationship took a turn to a more serious level during the Christmas break in December 1967. At what had now become a regular Saturday night movie, Kristine reached down and took Mark's hand. She held it for the entire movie. On the way home, Mark parked his father's car in the restaurant parking lot. Before they got out of the car, Mark reached over and pulled Kristine closer. It was only one kiss but at that point both came to the same conclusion that they may be destined to be together. The relationship never went beyond a kiss as Kristine was one of the nice girls and Mark remembered well the guidance that his mother gave his sister.

The last year of high school Mark developed into a mature, handsome man and Kristine into an attractive woman. Most of his friends already decided what they wanted to do in life. For Mark there was no firm idea what he wanted to do in university, never mind life. He always achieved great marks and was leaving secondary school with an 87 percent average, math being on the high side. He would be welcomed at any university in Canada. His father was a successful lawyer and hoped that Mark would follow his footsteps and eventually join him in partnership but Mark wasn't too keen to do this. Without a real vision for himself, he targeted an economics degree. As long as he needed an undergraduate degree, he might as well get something that could help make him rich. Mark's mother was a typical home maker as his dad had done well so she didn't have to work. She actually enjoyed being at home and doted on Mark until he left the family home in Regina for the campus at University of Toronto. U of T was considered one of the better post secondary schools with not just a full range of undergraduate degrees, but also many more career-focused graduate programs.

Kristine's heart was set on a history degree eventually going into teaching and her choice was Dalhousie in Halifax. The reality of their going in different directions was hard on both Mark and Kristine.

The last few weeks of August before heading off to university brought them a lot closer, both emotionally and physically, but neither was prepared to commit sexually. Mark vividly recalled one specific moment when his feelings overcame him and he asked Kristine for a promise that they see no one else. Filled with emotion, she kissed him like never before.

The time came for separation and both promised to see each other in Regina at the Christmas break. At the parting, tears were evident in four eyes and a farewell kiss was a kiss that both would remember for a long, long time.

Between September and October, they exchanged letters. The letters were far from love letters, rather an update on activities on their respective campuses. In a second letter from Mark he joked that there were a lot of young ladies vying for his time, but he was sticking to his promise to her. That letter went unanswered. He thought maybe she was upset with his comments or just bogged down with studies. As the Christmas break approached, Mark couldn't stop thinking about Kristine. He could still feel the softness of her lips as well as the tenderness of her young body as they embraced. He was anxious to get back to Regina and the long train ride home helped him reinforce his feelings for her. Perhaps she didn't know how he felt. Could it be that he needed to take the first step toward a more serious level and suggest a commitment? Yes, it was time.

As soon as he got in the front door, his mother and father hugged him. There were the usual twenty questions. How was his room? How was the food? What were his marks like? Did he choose a career yet? Janet sat in the corner grinning. She recently graduated from university in British Columbia and was home to begin her career as a veterinarian. She smiled as she went through the same questions in the past few years.

After the exchange of pleasantries, Mark went to his room to unpack. He looked around and for the first time, realized that his life was beyond this house. Yes, the memories would always be there, but he had grown out of the model airplanes on the shelf and the baseball bat and glove in the corner. He felt so mature and chuckled noticing that his mom put the galaxy of the universe bedspread on his bed. Elated, he saw that there was still a phone in his room. He picked it up and called Kristine's house and Kristine's mother answered.

"Hello Mrs. Locke, its Mark Hiott. Merry Christmas. I hope you and the family are well."

"Hello Mark. It's great to hear from you. Yes, we are all well. How is school going?"

"It's going as well as I expected. I still haven't made a career decisions yet, but it will come. Mrs. Locke. I was wondering, is Kristine there?"

"No, Kristine isn't here. We're so disappointed that she has decided to stay in Halifax over Christmas. You may know that she has been spending her free time volunteering in an outreach program for the needy. She called two weeks ago and told us that she was staying in Halifax to help out over the holidays."

There was a long pause. "Well, thank you Mrs. Locke. If she calls, let her know we spoke."

Mark sat back thinking hard. The thoughts of taking the relationship to a more serious level evaporated. In Kristine's letter in October she said she would see Mark at Christmas. Why wouldn't she let him know? No doubt there was someone else in her life. Mark brooded for a couple of hours not sure if his flip comment had pushed her away or did she find someone else. By the time dinner was being served, his insides were churning. What could have happened?

After the Christmas break, Mark reached out one more time to Kristine by letter. Again, no response. It was over. He now knew he must put aside his feelings for her and concentrate on finishing his first year strong.

When he did go home for breaks, the only news was that Kristine was still at Dalhousie and still very much involved in an outreach program.

Chapter 5

During years two and three at university, Mark went on a few dates, but nothing serious. He dedicated most of his free time swimming and in non-academic clubs, especially the Theatre Club. Theater was a way to get back to his youth when he liked being able to use his imagination and be another person. It was also a way to escape his reputation as a quiet reserved young man with an introverted personality.

As the end of year three approached, he was desperately trying to determine what he wanted to do. He already decided to go for an honours degree which would take him through year four, but time was running out to apply for a Masters degree. A letter from his father again suggested that he consider law. The letter sat on his desk in his room as a reminder that he must make a decision soon.

He didn't have to wait long and it came like a lightning bolt in October 1972 at a Theatre Club meeting. The topic that night was projecting the voice. On stage was Reverend Paul Morris, the current Minister at the Christian Reformed Ministries at the University. His reputation as a powerful and compelling speaker from the pulpit was widely known on campus, so he was a natural to be a club guest. That night, he chose to use series of demonstrations for dramatic voice control. As a script, he recited passages from the Bible and after each demonstration Morris would ask one of the students to read a selected passage. Instructions were to use punctuation and pauses for effect and to stress key words such as 'you' or 'us' to engage the audience. Above all, they needed to connect with the audience through eye contact and gestures. The first three participants did a great job and received vigorous rounds of applause. Mark sat knowing that his turn was coming and as usual sweating, getting dry in the throat and having a hard time controlling a quivering lip. Mark heard his name being called and he slowly rose accepting the Bible from Morris. The Bible was opened to Proverbs. Mark read through the words to himself first, then slowly put his head up and began to recite the verse. After only a dozen words, the audience was staring at Mark. He felt no nervousness and had no difficulty doing what was asked. He was in total command. The delivery was exceptional and very few in the audience weren't mesmerized by Marks' passion and captivating performance. In fact, as the words came out of his mouth he never felt so comfortable. He could have gone on for hours. After his turn, he received a loud and long round of applause from the rest of the club members. Morris smiled broadly and gave him a pat on the back.

Strangely, Mark became more unengaged in the rest of demonstrations as the evening went on, but not the specific words that were being spoken. It was the message in the verses that Mark heard so very well; the beauty in the Psalms, the lessons in Peter and Paul and the comfort he felt. It was as if a light went off in his heart.

After the exercises that evening, Mark excitedly approached Morris and asked if there was any time the next day to speak.

Mark didn't sleep that night and was at Morris' office a half hour before his appointment time.

"Come in Mark. I know I said this last night, but your effort was exceptional."

"Thank you Reverend Morris."

"Please call me Paul. So Mark, what can I do for you?"

Mark got to the point very quickly telling Morris that he never felt inspiration as he did hearing the words from the Bible. He entered university with no real profession in mind and picked economics as a fail-safe career, but really wasn't committed yet and was wrestling with a dilemma. In fact, up until last night, he was still searching for his life. Although he was raised in a Christian family and attended Church, Mark recalled the Sunday morning's in Sunday school relating those times as more social than inspiring. He never considered himself a strong religious person, but the Bible's words ignited a new feeling in Mark, so much so that he spent the better part of the night reading the Bible. Each passage, each verse was a revelation for Mark. Why was this happening now? He wanted and needed to know what advice Morris could give him.

Morris smiled through Mark's words and when Mark was finished, Morris rose and walked to the window before turning and addressing the young man.

"Mark, you are strongly attracted to the scriptures and this may be an option for you. I don't know your background or your experiences, but you are still at a point in your life to make a decision that could have a wonderful effect on you as well as so many others. You came here for advice so here it is. I suggest you finish your undergraduate degree and begin a Masters of Divinity. If you like the path, ordination could follow. Notice I said 'could' because it may still not be clear what you want to do. If you did decide on ordination, this path would take you to a life of peace, a life of support for people, and a life of comfort for you and your family. If you do not like that path, you still have lots of time to change direction to another career. But perhaps the best advice I can give you is this. You have one life to live. Will it be the life you want to live, the life you could live, or the life you should live? The best result is all three, but again, it is up to you."

Mark immediately returned to his room and completed the application to enter the Master of Divinity program at Knox College.

The Christmas trip home that year was a mix between reading more of the Bible and trying to figure out how he would tell his parents of his career choice. To say that his news would be surprising was an understatement but he wasn't concerned as he knew he made the right choice.

As he walked up the walkway, his father threw open the door and grabbed him by the shoulders.

"Mark, it is so good to see you. Look at you. Come on in."

"Hi Dad. It's good to be home. Where are Mom and Janet?"

"They are out shopping. Your mother has been in a real tizzy since the engagement. Planning for the wedding and the reception has taken a lot of her time, and I am sure, will take a lot of my money."

"Dad, I can see by the look on your face that you are enjoying it as well. I am so happy for Janet. Her fiancée seems to be a very nice guy and you must be elated given that he is a lawyer. You two will have a great time, that's for sure."

"Yes Mark, Russ is a lawyer, and a fine one at that."

"Dad, I was wondering if we can have a chat before they get home."

"Sounds serious. Sure, let's sit down. Would you like a beer?"

"No thanks Dad." Mark sat on the wing chair facing his father directly. He needed to see the reaction. "I have made a decision regarding my career."

"That's wonderful. So don't keep me in suspense. What have you decided?"

"I am going into the Ministry."

"You are going to work for the government? Which Ministry?"

"No, Dad, religion. I want to be a Minister."

The room was silent for several seconds. "Well, that is a bit of a shock. What compelled you to make this decision?"

Mark related the revelation he experienced at the Theatre Club and how he was stirred inside and that feeling hasn't left him. He felt a very strong attraction to scripture and Christian values and wanted to give religious studies a try for at least one year. After all, he was still young enough to change his mind and have a good career. He was, however very unlikely to change. It was something that he wanted to do, could do, and should do.

"Well son, you have thought this out. I have always known you would find your way. Being a Minister is a fine and honourable profession. You know you have my support. I guess you'll be doing the blessing at dinner from now on." Mark's father rose from the couch and walked over to Mark and shook his hand.

****

After his first year in theological college, Mark was near the top of his class. In year two of three, he began supply work and quickly gained a reputation for his preaching and connectivity to people. Paul Morris sat in the front row at Mark's graduation with a proud look on his face. Mark searched out Morris at the reception.

"Paul, I'm glad you could make it."

"Congratulations Mark. I must admit, I have listened to a lot of undergraduate students that thought they might choose the ministry, but I felt from our first meeting that you would make it."

"Thanks Paul."

"Any idea what is next for you, perhaps a PhD?"

"Not yet. I want to get my own charge then look at a doctorate."

"I think that is a good move."

"I have been watching the vacancies in the past few months and there are a couple that interest me."

"Well, if you need a reference, I'd be pleased to give you one."

It was no surprise that he was called to the pulpit in November 1975 to Shoreside Presbyterian Church in Moncton, New Brunswick. It was a small charge outside of the city proper that couldn't afford a seasoned veteran and needed new energy. Shoreside was an older Church with a white clapboard exterior and a wall mounted plaque saying 'Established 1898'. Inside, his office was small but functional and in very good condition considering nineteen Minister's names were engraved on a plaque outside the narthex.

There were less than one hundred families on the role, many of them seniors. On any given Sunday, about fifty adults and five children came to Church. The choir of seven were better than he thought they would be. A volunteer secretary worked two mornings a week, one of those days preparing a simple one page Sunday calendar.

The community was slowly beginning to turn over as younger families were moving into the area trying to escape the housing costs in the city. As a result, some of the smaller manufacturing companies were also relocating to avoid increased taxation. Mark soon found out that as a young single man, there was no shortage of overly friendly women at the coffee hour after service, and at least one invitation a month to dinner to meet the single daughter or niece. Each time this happened, a brief memory of Kristine came back and he often wondered what happened to her. He heard very little about her from his family so she wasn't in Regina. He guessed she graduated and went somewhere to work, or possible get married. Oh well, he thought, Kristine was another lifetime and it was her that cut off their relationship.

The first year went very well for Mark. He was able to accomplish a lot of outreach and grow attendance. His sermons were more reflective of life and less of a Bible study. This was refreshing for all attendees and something that they hoped for when they called a newly ordained and young Minister. The pews were filling up and Sunday school added eight new children. To the delight of the Board of Managers, the Church was looking at a balanced budget the following year for the first time in a decade. His never ending support and attendance for the various bazaars and events was welcomed by all Church groups. In addition, he became very popular in the community, often volunteering to help reclamation projects for the heritage society. Throughout the year, he corresponded with Morris back at the University of Toronto and Morris was delighted that Mark to see Marks' success. Mark felt extra comfort that Morris was there to turn to if there were any issues he needed advice with.

****

It was Sunday September 22, 1977, a date he would never forget. Mark put the final touches on both the children's story and his sermon the night before, so there was some extra time that morning to do a pre-service stroll through the sanctuary. He heard that many in the congregation expressed their appreciation for this as some couldn't get to coffee hour to have a few words with their Minister. He especially liked to chat with the people that he knew were having challenges, hoping that his direct contact would make them feel a bit better. Today, there was a new family of four attending and he spent a bit more time with them. As he turned and continued to walk down the centre aisle smiling and shaking hands, he glanced towards the entrance to the Church. He froze. He stared at a beautiful woman with dark auburn hair and deep green eyes. She stared back with a slight smile on her face. Slowly, he walked toward her.

"Kristine?"

"Yes, Mark, it's me."

She reached out to shake his hand and he held her hand longer than his usual grip. She was still trim and dressed smartly. He stared at her face, a pretty face that changed little over the years. Still holding her hand, he realized that a few people near the door were looking at them wondering who this woman was. He let go and fumbling for words, Mark threw out an obligatory statement. "It's so good to see you. Are you staying for the service?"

"Yes, I am Mark. Actually, I was hoping that we could talk later?"

"Yes, yes, by all means. After the service, I usually spend a few minutes at the door while some people leave. Most go to our coffee hour and I join then. Just follow the crowd for coffee and I will see you there."

Mark opened the service with prayer before sitting to listen to the Duty Elder deliver the announcements. He noticed that Kristine took a seat with a full view of Mark whether he was sitting or standing. Mark's children's story and sermon focussed on joy.

He was always close to that word and today it seemed to have even more meaning. During the service Mark would gaze throughout the congregation. Each time he looked in Kristine's direction, she would widen her smile. Near the end of the service when the collection was being taken up, he recalled the last time they saw each other, and of course, the kiss. He reminded himself that was eight years ago and no doubt, Kristine moved on from Mark. There was probably someone else in her life. He wasn't sure to look forward to or dread seeing her after the service.

At coffee hour, and much more relaxed, Mark approached Kristine just as one of the members was leaving her.

"Hi Kristine, glad you stayed for a coffee. I would imagine that some of the folks have been more than welcoming. They tend to pounce, and I mean really pounce on any new face that graces our small Church."

"Yes, Mark. They made me feel extremely welcome. They have a lot of very nice words to say about you. Your youth, your energy, your skill, and your commitment are something that they were missing before you arrived."

"It is a wonderful congregation. I have been blessed. "

After another awkward silence, Mark said, "You asked if we could talk. Let's go to my office for some privacy."

In his office, they sat not saying anything for a full minute. He couldn't help but stare at her. She developed into a beautiful woman. He could smell the same British soap that she used as a teenager and that he liked so very much. Mark fought off not only the good memories but also the hurt when she drifted away.

"Kristine. How have you been? What are you doing now? I have so many questions."

"Mark, I need to say something. I am very sorry that I didn't connect with you after our first semester at university. I owed you more than neglecting your letters. There are no excuses except that I got pretty wrapped up in our outreach program. You must think I'm terrible. Please forgive me."

Mark couldn't put his finger on it, but he sensed that there was more to her being in his Church than to come and apologize. "No forgiveness is required Kristine. We all get wrapped up from time to time. My sister Janet sent me a letter a few months ago telling me that you were in Regina working. You didn't come all the way to Moncton to apologize, did you?"

"There is more to it than that. It's a long story, one that I feel you deserve to hear. Do you want to hear it?"

"Sure. Let me get a couple of coffees."

Kristine sipped her coffee and began by telling Mark that her goal to become a history teacher didn't pan out. Her marks weren't good enough so she transferred into a political science degree with a minor in French. At Dalhousie she participated in the usual activities including playing inter-mural volleyball, joining a sorority and found volunteering for outreach programs she found very satisfying. Kristine also joined a club called the Allegorists, a club discussing myths from all over the world. Her real focus was, however, the outreach program for the under-housed and homeless in Halifax where she spent virtually all her free time in the program, including Christmas' at shelters serving food. It was the volunteering that kept her from returning to Regina for holidays and vacation. After graduation in 1972, she volunteered for one year of international aid in French Guiana. It was an interesting time and she learned a lot.

"What made it interesting?"

"French Guiana is a country full of superstitions and legends. Having some understanding from my Allegorists group in university, it was an eye opener to hear some of this first hand from the locals."

Kristine continued, telling Mark she went on to work for an agency for the addicted in Montreal for a few years but got homesick and went back to Regina to restart life. That is when she got a call from Ann Haggarty at the Nester Agency in Moncton begging her to join her as a program coordinator. It seemed like a natural fit. It was an outreach agency, she would be working for a friend, and French was one of two languages spoken. Her experience in Montreal was a great assist.

"Yes, I have heard of that agency. They do some good work with the under-housed and homeless. Ann spoke at a town meeting last year. She seems quite passionate. How did she know you were in Regina?"

"Agencies exist in a small world in Canada. She probably saw my name on a directory, tracked me down and called. That's about the whole story."

"Quite the adventure Kristine. Oh, I should have said that I was sorry to hear about your father's passing."

"Thank you."

"How is your Mom?"

"She is getting by with friends and her hobbies."

"I guess she was happy to see you come home."

"Yes, but Mom wasn't too happy with me for a while. I think it was my choice of a career. There isn't a lot of opportunity to climb the ladder in the not-for-profit industry and the pay tends to be on the low side. That's life but a life that I really enjoy."

"Well, that is what counts. "

After another long silence, Mark spoke. "Kristine, how did you find me?"

"I knew from your sister that you were a man of the cloth in Moncton. Shortly after I arrived, I saw your name on an advertisement for one of your Church suppers. I had to come and see if it was the same Mark Hiott that I knew."

"As far as I know, I am the only Mark Hiott in Moncton."

"Mark, I must say that I was a bit surprised that you are a Minister. I don't recall a passion for this when we were in high school. I thought you were heading for something in the financial world."

"It surprised me too. Let's just say it was an act of God."

They both laughed.

Kristine looked at Mark then lowered her face slightly. "Is there a Mrs. Hiott?"

"No. I did have a serious relationship that started in my second year at university, but once I decided to go into the ministry, she felt she wanted more in life. Since then I haven't had a lot of time to date. And besides, a Minister has to be more than just discrete."

"How about you? Married, engaged?"

"There was a short relationship at university with a lacrosse player but like you, I didn't have a lot of time. After graduation, I dated a few times but between travel and the long hours, dating wasn't a priority. You don't meet a lot of the marrying type when you work the streets. Most of the men are broken one way or the other. To be very honest Mark, I never forgot you."

Mark squinted his eyes and sat back and absorbed the comment. First the question about a girl friend or wife, then getting to the, 'I never forgot you' comment. What was her real motivation for coming here? He sensed that her visit was more an apology for that first Christmas when she did not come home from University. He needed time to think this through and more time with her to sort out his questions.

"Kristine, I have a family to visit this afternoon. Can I treat you to dinner tonight and we can catch up?"

"That would be great Mark, or should I call you Reverend Hiott?"

"No, Kristine, Mark is just fine. Can you meet me at Paul's Bistro on Maple Street at 6:00?"

"See you there Mark."

As they stood up and went to the door of his office, he stared into those deep green eyes, smiled and reached out to shake her hand. She avoided the handshake and, instead, reached for Mark and they had a very brief embrace.

Mark met with a family that afternoon but his mind was drifting back to Kristine, her words, and the embrace.

Chapter 6

Although it wasn't yet October, the cool wind and drizzle were announcing winter. Mark arrived at five minutes to six and Kristine was already sitting at a table waiting for him. As he approached, she rose and the two shared another short embrace.

"Have you been waiting long Kristine?"

"No, I arrived only a minute or two before you. It's good that we got here at 6:00. The weather looks like it could get nasty tonight."

The restaurant was warm and dry and table candles threw off a warm glow and set a certain mood for the dinner. Both ordered a glass of wine and the steak sandwich special.

"Kristine, I recall that you weren't a meat eater in high school.

"After years of soup, soup and more soup, I've turned into a steak gal."

Over dinner, the conversation became very comfortable. Kristine began by describing how the altruistic life took over thanks largely to her exposure in Halifax. It made her feel good to help people and she saw this as a real calling for her.

"You said earlier that you were an aid worker in French Guiana. What was that like?"

Kristine hesitated before responding. "It was hot and humid."

"What did you do there?"

"We helped build houses in remote villages and when that was finished, we assisted farmers bringing crops in."

"That sounds exciting. Why didn't you continue working as an international aid worker?"

"Just wasn't for me. The food was different, we slept on cots in tents and as I said, the weather. I never thought I would miss snow."

"What was Montreal like?"

"The work was tougher and more dangerous than Halifax, especially for women. For me, it was a chance to get a foothold back in Canada with an agency."

Kristine went on to describe working as a part time agency worker in Regina when she returned home. Just by accident, she bumped into Mark's sister one day and found out that he went beyond his undergrad and was now in the Ministry down east. She repeated what she told Mark earlier that day getting a call from Ann Haggarty asking her if she wanted a job. She arrived in Moncton a few months living in an apartment on the other side of town.

"Mark, that's enough about me. How about you? You said it was an act of God. How did that happen?"

Mark told her of his road to Shoreside, starting with his meeting with Morris at the University of Toronto. He wasn't married, not for the lack of trying by the ladies in the Church. They laughed. He was content in his role and was looking forward to a long life in the Ministry. He was well aware that Ministers usually spent seven or eight years in one place, so he saw himself a few more years in Moncton before any consideration to move on. But then again, it really wasn't up to him as there was the, 'Call'.

"A 'Call'?"

It took Mark a few minutes to explain that the Call doesn't come by telephone; it comes from the highest authority.

"Mark, are you happy with your choices?"

"Absolutely."

Twice during dinner Kristine patted Marks arm lightly in the funnier moments as if it was an extension of her laugh. He also noticed that her eyes seldom left his and the smile was almost permanent on her face. As the dinner came to an end, Mark looked hard at Kristine and the emotion of that good bye kiss so many years ago flooded back.

"Kristine, how did you get here tonight?"

"I took a taxi."

"It's raining pretty hard now. I have my car. Let me give you a lift."

The ride was only six blocks and not a lot was said. He stopped in front of her building and she reached over with her left hand and squeezed his forearm.

"Mark, I so enjoyed tonight. Maybe we can do it again sometime."

"That would be nice."

Kristine took one last look at Mark, and darted through the rain to the front door of her building. She stopped at the door, turned, and waved at Mark before disappearing inside.

****

Monday and Tuesday Mark worked on his sermon at home but kept thinking about Kristine. The nagging questions were a mixture of 'whys'. Why was she really here in Moncton? Why did she track him down? Why did she say 'I never forgot you'? Unsure what to do, he decided to take his own advice to many people that came to him for guidance. 'When presented with a dilemma, confront it.'

Late Tuesday afternoon, he called the Nester Agency asking for Kristine. She was out so he left a message with the agency receptionist. Twenty minutes later, his phone rang.

"Mark, its Kristine Locke, you called?"

"Hi Kristine. I was wondering if you are you available tomorrow for dinner."

"Mark, I can't do tomorrow. That is the night we have a drop in session for the homeless. How is Thursday?"

"Great. Can I pick you up at 6:30?"

Kristine was waiting in front of her building as Mark drove up to the front door.

"Roadhouse okay for you? They have everything from hamburgers to seafood, and something special for a steak gal."

"Sounds great Mark."

Dinner was more a date than an information session. They reminisced about high school days and some of their old friends. They talked about local politics and community issues and even about a few world news items. Again, Kristine patted Marks arms a few times.

"You know Kristine, being single I cook a lot and I have been trying to cook the perfect steak for years. What would you suggest?"

"I think it's the combination of the spices and the heat. Enough salt, pepper and garlic, high heat and seven minutes a side is medium."

"Perhaps I'll give that a try."

"I would love to try one of your steaks."

"Kristine, you asked me Sunday night if I was happy with my choices. How about you?"

"I could have done a few things differently but that's all water under the bridge now. I'm enjoying my new life."

Mark wasn't sure if he should pursue 'I could have done a few things differently but that's all water under the bridge now'. He decided to leave it alone.

After dinner Mark drove to Kristine's apartment building. He got out of the car and walked around to open the door for her. The same feeling that was there so many years ago flooded back and their goodnight embrace turned into a light kiss.

****

That evening, Mark's mind was in another world. His counselling training while studying for his Masters in Divinity was to look at things deeply and ask only the pertinent questions. So here he is, far, far away from Regina, and after years, Kristine drops in. There wasn't a lot of detail about her time in French Guiana or Montreal. She was recruited for a job in the same city where he lives. Her life isn't as fulfilled as she wanted, but she likes what she does. She is very attractive yet there is no one special in her life. Could there be more, he wondered? He stopped the 'whys' in his head and focussed on his feelings for her, feelings that far outweighed the questions.

The next six months were a whirlwind of romance. Kristine became a regular at the Sunday service helping every chance she could and the ladies in the Church were thrilled that he found somebody, especially someone so very helpful in the Church's programs. She fit in as she hoped.

The wedding one year after Kristine appeared at Mark's church was a traditional community affair with every pew in the Church occupied. The ladies Guild went beyond expectations with floral displays spanning the front of the Church. The Church Secretary prepared a grand order of service that included a picture of the engaged couple on the back. Mark picked the music and the Choir, now twenty strong, was in full harmony. Mark and Kristine agreed that one of the Ministers from the Presbytery would preside. In the front row were Kristine's mother, Mark's parents, his sister Janet and his brother-in-law Russ. The service was followed by a buffet in the lower hall for one hundred and twenty put on by the ladies. The traditional speeches were mixed with humour and seriousness and highlighted by Kristine's mother who's pride and happiness dripping off every word.

After a short honeymoon in Florida, Rev. and Mrs. Hiott settled into a routine life in Moncton. With two salaries, they decided to build a small house in the parish. Children were discussed, but it turned out that Kristine was not able to bear a child. They decided to consider adoption down the road. For now, all was well.

As the years went by at Shoreside, Mark and Kristine often talked about Mark's next Church but he knew it must be a 'Call'. It didn't take long. His Call was to Mountaincrest Presbyterian Church in Hamilton, Ontario. Although they established a comfortable life in Moncton, the move offered a number of advantages, including a larger congregation, more money, more opportunity for Kristine to follow her desires, and Hamilton was closer to their homes in Regina.

Chapter 7

Mountaincrest was as warm and welcoming as the Church in New Brunswick. Over the next six fast paced years, Mark continued to find success and was able to grow the Sunday school substantially to the point that the congregation approved a paid youth director to assist Mark with the children. Kristine wasted no time finding employment as an Administrator at a not-for-profit. Coming from Moncton, housing was more expensive in Hamilton, but the Trustees retained a manse and were able to conclude a lease and allow Mark and Kristine to occupy the property. It was a classic brownstone two story with turn of the century craftsmanship reflected in every room. The house was large and an ideal place to host dinners and small events. This was something where Kristine excelled and their time in Hamilton became a wonderful experience both socially and career wise.

But his birthday dinner in March 1988 changed Mark's life forever.

Now two months after the accident that took Kristine's life and injured Mark, his physical wounds healed but there was a deep emptiness inside of Mark. The truck driver's company settlement was substantial, but could not replace Kristine.

Russ finalized the will and that sat on Mark's desk in his study at home. A few days after it arrived, he found time to open it and read through the changes that Russ completed. Everything looked good so he went to the bedroom closet to retrieve the document box and store his will. He remembered the small unmarked white envelope that blocked Kristine's will that last time he was in the box. He pulled it out before putting his will inside and carried the envelope to his desk before slicing it open. Inside was a one page folded note. Immediately, he recognized the writing as Kristine's and felt a lump in his throat. Carefully, he read the note, put it on the desk for several minutes, picked it up and read it again.

'Mark, if you are reading this, I am gone. First and most important, please know that I loved you very much. The memory of our first kiss at Christmas in 1967 was what brought me to you so many years later. Seems so childish to say that, but it is the truth. Looking for and finding you again made me realize that I was capable of living the life I wanted to live. There was, however, a period in my life that could have been better. It was between the end of university and my arrival in Moncton. You need not know the details; suffice to say that I learned that family and friends are more important than riches. I hope that you will remember only the good times we enjoyed and that you will continue to provide Christian leadership for your flock. Please know that I loved you more than anything else in this world. Kristine.'

Mark re-read the letter twice more before putting it back in the envelope and dropping it into his desk drawer. Over the next several days, he pulled it out and re-read it zeroing in on certain words that he was having difficulty with. First the phrase, *'Looking for and finding you.'* Looking for him? Their reuniting wasn't as Kristine said originally? She actually planned the reunion - she tracked him down? *'I was capable of living the life I wanted to live.'* That took Mark back to the critical decision point when he met Rev. Paul Morris. How ironic that she used these words. *'A period in my life that could have been better.'* What did she mean by that? Was there something that she did that she was ashamed of? Was there another man? So many questions.

Each day was difficult. The words in Kristine's note kept reverberating in his head. Writing his sermons became difficult and the good times at the events were not as good anymore. The house was an empty reminder of her and each day the silence in the four walls was deafening. He made a note to speak to the Church Trustees about leaving the manse and finding a condominium, a place with no memories.

The pain in the next few months was softened by a loving congregation, a heavy workload, a new residence and more importantly, his faith in God remained and he continued to hope that time would heal him. Time also helped him slowly erase the words in Kristine's note. There was nothing he could do about it anyway; she was gone.

In mid July, Mark took Kristine's ashes to Regina and performed a private family interment. It was the right time for the families to get together, just long enough after the funeral. Everyone accepted Kristine's loss and the burial was more a celebration of life. The time also let everyone know how well Mark was coping.

After a family dinner that evening, Mrs. Locke pulled Mark aside.

"Mark, I want to tell you that you are the very best son-in-law I could have ever hoped for. Kristine's life was cut short, far too short, but you made her life so worthwhile. Thank you."

"Mrs. Locke, we both wanted her for many more years. I can only thank God for the time we did have together."

Mark and Mrs. Locke shared an embrace.

"Mrs. Locke, Kristine wanted you to have this. It was a watch she bought while she was university."

Mrs. Locke caressed the watch in her hands and thanked Mark.

"Mark, I almost forgot. Since your wedding, I shipped all of her belongings to her in Moncton and Hamilton. Last week I was cleaning out a drawer and found this envelope full of photos. See, French Guiana is written on it. Perhaps you would like them."

Mark took the package of photos and thanked Mrs. Locke.

By October, seven months after the accident, Mark was well settled into his condominium, dwelling on the reminders of his life with Kristine including their wedding picture and some souvenirs from their honeymoon. The Polaroid photos that Mrs. Locke gave him were on top of Kristine's note in his desk drawer. He pulled them out again, rereading the note and glancing through photos. The dozen pictures were scenic shots, some with paths, and others with rivers and a few with mountain tops. On the back were the numbers from one to twelve. He put them back in the drawer.

****

The day before Halloween, Mark's phone rang.

"Hello."

"Hello, is this Reverend Mark Hiott?"

"Yes it is."

"It's Sid Forrest. You remember that my wife and I bought your house in Moncton."

"Sid, yes, how are you doing?"

"Fine. More importantly, how are you doing? We heard about Mrs. Hiott. What a shame."

"As you can imagine Sid, things have changed a lot in my life. It's a lonely time, much lonelier than I could ever have anticipated. Fortunately, I have a wonderful congregation and friends here in Hamilton."

"Once again Reverend Hiott, our condolences."

"Thank you. To what do I owe this call?"

"Mrs. Forrest and I started to do a bit of renovation to the house. You folks did a marvellous job building it and we thought we would add a few rooms, you know toward the bush side where there is lots of room."

"That's interesting Sid. We had a plan to do the same if we stayed there."

"Well, one of the walls that needed to be removed was the wall between the master bedroom and the hallway."

"Yes, I remember it well. It had the dark wallpaper that Kristine loved."

"Yes, that's the one. When our contractor was removing it, he found a small leather pouch in the air return with the name Kristine in it. We thought that it might be something you folks put in there - something like a time capsule. We didn't open it and would like to mail it to you. I wanted to make sure that I had the right person. Where can I send it?"

"Well, Sid, it wouldn't be a time capsule. Perhaps something that Kristine put in there and forgot about. Send it to my office, Mountaincrest Presbyterian Church."

"Yes, I have the address."

"Thank you for the call and give my regards to Mrs. Forrest."

It was the following Tuesday when the parcel arrived. Mark unwrapped it and sat in his easy chair in his office looking at the leather pouch. The name Kristine looked like it had been etched in with a sharp knife. What if it was something that would remind him of Kristine? What if it was a gift for him that she forgot about? He undid the snap and looked inside then let the contents drop onto his desk. There were only two things; an identification card from a company called TDM, and an eight sided ring. He stared at the picture on the card. It was Kristine, but the name was Paulette Darion. Her hair was quite short. Was this a joke? Why the eight sided finger ring?

Mark spent a sleepless night thinking that he never knew his wife as well as he thought. The note that Kristine left was mystery enough, but now these articles that made no sense at all. He was, however, smart enough to know that the note and items were linked. How would he get to the bottom of this, if ever?

Chapter 8

On a frigid Hamilton morning, Harold Fresher sat near the back of Mountaincrest Presbyterian Church reflecting on two changes that now defined his life. The first was leaving tenure at Royal Military College in Kingston, a teaching career that he thought would be his life. After all, he was very qualified with an under graduate degree from Algoma University in Sault Ste. Marie where he majored in History then at Dalhousie for a Masters Degree in Military Studies followed by his PhD in World Conflicts from The University of Toronto. The second was the success he enjoyed when he took on a cold case for the Canadian Forces National Investigation Service. That propelled him into establishing his own investigative services company in Hamilton less than three months ago. As good luck would have it, he already served two clients. Case one was a rich family wanting him to track down their daughter who ran from the Church and jilted some poor guy waiting at the altar. They didn't want the police involved as that would have been embarrassing. It wasn't a hard case as she drove off in her car that Fresher located in Oshawa two days later and spent a couple of hours convincing her to go home and sort things out as an adult. Case two was a large construction firm with a missing grader worth a half million dollars. The police didn't give this case a priority in a city with a high crime rate. It took a week, but the repainted grader was found in a competition company's yard. Once Fresher reported back to the rightful owner, the grader was returned along with a cash settlement to avoid charges.

The success in both cases and the fees from the two clients helped him establish his office and hire a secretary Samid. Samid graduated Police Foundations but tore a retina in training and decided to avoid policing as a career. To Fresher, Samid was a real find. He was very professional, thorough, and treated his job seriously. When Fresher left the office Friday, there were three appointments for him early the next week. Samid told him that they were all referrals. Great, he thought, the best form of advertising.

He sat in the pew feeling very good about himself and doing a bit of daydreaming. Fresher, Harold Fresher didn't have quite the same ring as Bond, James Bond. He chuckled inside. As he sat enjoying the quiet hum of the congregation before the service started, the background organ music was quite soothing and felt more relaxed than he did in quite a few weeks but he could feel the eyes of the regulars staring at him mumbling in low voices wondering who the new man was.

From behind a voice brought him back to reality.

"Good morning. I'm Mark Hiott, Minister here at Mountaincrest Presbyterian. Are you visiting?"

"I just moved to town and haven't had a chance yet to plant my faith roots anywhere."

"Well, we would be more than glad to help you with that."

"Thanks Reverend Hiott. I may take you up on it.'

"Sorry, I should have introduced myself. I'm Harold Fresher."

"Welcome Mr. Fresher. We have a coffee hour after Church. Hopefully you will join us."

Mark found Fresher after the service at coffee hour. Fresher was enduring the usual welcoming committee being all over him when Mark came to his rescue.

"Mr. Fresher. I hope you enjoyed the service. Perhaps it helped with the faith roots issue."

"Please call me Harold. Here is my business card."

"Dr. Fresher? Medical or dental?"

"Neither. I should tell you that I found the sermon topical and to the point, especially the reference to finding one's way."

"Why so?"

"I just opened up my investigation services company here in Hamilton a couple of weeks ago and it's always nice to be able to find one's way, especially in a city with so many one way streets." They both laughed.

Mark straightened up and asked, "A doctor with an Investigation Services company?"

"Yes. I have a Masters and PhD in the field."

Mark's facial expression shifted to a more serious nature. Without any hesitation, he seized the opportunity that was in front of him.

"Harold, I have a situation that I would like to discuss with you. Would you have any time tomorrow?"

"Sounds serious."

"I'm not sure. All I know is that my late wife left me with a mystery that I cannot solve"

"Reverend, can you drop into my office around 10:00? My address is on the card."

"Please call me Mark. Yes, I will see you there."

Puzzled by Mark's request, Fresher left the Church wondering why a Minister might need him.

****

On Monday morning, Samid was already in the office with coffee waiting for Fresher.

"Samid, Reverend Mark Hiott from Mountaincrest Presbyterian is coming by at 10:00. Can you do a quick check and see if there is anything I should know about him?"

"Sure. Remember that your first appointment is coming in for 11:00."

A half an hour later, Samid went into Fresher's office.

"Harold, the only thing I found out was that he has been in Hamilton for two years. He has a very good reputation in the community. Earlier this year, his wife was killed in a car accident. A truck went through a red light. There isn't much more. That's about it."

"Thank you Samid. When he arrives, please show him in."

At 9:55, Samid announced Mark's arrival.

"Hello Harold. Thank you very much for seeing me so soon."

"Hi Mark. Come on in. Let me pour you a coffee. You met my assistant Samid out front. He found this Sumatra blend. I lived on coffee in university, but never tasted anything like this. Cream and sugar? "

"Black please." Mark sipped the hot liquid. "Harold, this is excellent coffee. I may drop in from time to time and beg a cup."

"Any time Mark."

"Harold, what got you into this business?"

"That is a long story but I don't think you are here to listen to me. What is on your mind? I sensed something yesterday when I could see your whole demeanour change when you realized what I did for a living. What can I help you with?"

"I'm not sure where to start."

"In this business, you always start at the beginning."

Mark spent the next hour going through the last several years beginning with the first time he met Kristine in grade nine.

Harold was taking notes as Mark spoke.

- Met Kristine Locke in 1964 - grade 9
- Nothing between them until Dec 1967
- More serious as high school ending
- Both off to university in fall of 1969 - Mark to U of T - Kristine to Dal
- Kristine not home for Christmas first year - 1969
- Kristine accepted job from sorority sister in Moncton June 1977
- Couple reunited in Moncton Sept 1977
- Married May 1978
- Built house 1981
- Moved to Hamilton 1986
- Kristine killed March 1988
- Note for Mark - very confusing – found July 1988
- Pouch with ID - TDM - not her name on ID - eight sided ring - arrived Oct 1988, seven months after death
- Paulette Darion?

"Mark, any idea where Kristine was between 1969 and 1977 or what this TDM is?"

"Well, she took a three year degree program at university, graduated in 1972 and went off to French Guiana on a one year international aid tour.. After that, she came home for a very brief visit, and then took a job in Montreal at an agency for the addicted. She was there for close to four years coming home only for her father's funeral. My sister did see her in Regina after the work in Montreal. The next I heard or saw of her is when she came to my Church in Moncton. She seldom spoke of those years except to say that she was helping people and I didn't ask too many questions. I am of little help beyond that, especially the reference to TDM. I just assumed that it may be an abbreviation for the agency she worked for. Here Harold. I brought along the note and the pouch with the ID and the ring."

Fresher read the note then picked up the ID card and the ring.

"Mark, is that her picture on the ID card?"

"Yes, but in high school and when we met in Moncton, her hair was long auburn not cropped like the photo."

"Did you ever see Kristine wear this ring?"

"No."

The next few seconds, Mark fidgeted with Fresher observing him closely.

"Mark, what is really bothering you."

After a long pause, Hiott said, "Harold, I feel somehow that my marriage was something that Kristine orchestrated for her purpose. Don't get me wrong, I think that our relationship morphed into love during the courtship, but I feel so confused and let down. I must admit that I never asked any deep questions of Kristine regarding the period between university and Moncton. I guess you would call it being smitten."

"Mark, as I said, I really need to start at the beginning and as I see it, which would be Sept 1969 when she went out of your life. I understand that her mother told you that she graduated in 1972, and those years in university may provide some information."

Fresher continued to probe for information, especially the way that Kristine got to Moncton and just happened to see Mark's name in the local paper. This was more than interesting given that Kristine was back in Canada after the French Guiana stint but was home only once in almost four years, for her father's funeral. There were a few questions that needed to be answered, mostly around Kristine's time in Montreal. Mark confirmed that he and Kristine were never in Montreal together. In fact, Mark was there only twice, first in 1969 when he was considering McGill as a possible university, and then again in 1976 at a Ministerial conference.

"Do you have any idea why she would have a second identity, Paulette Darion?"

"No, none what so ever."

"Do you think it could be a put on? I have seen those fake ID's as part of a game."

"No, Harold. Given all the mystery, I think it is real."

"Did Kristine speak French?"

"We took it in high school and she minored in it at university."

"Any idea what the ring is all about? Could this be some elaborate joke?"

"No idea regarding the ring, and yes, I do hope it's all an elaborate joke."

"You answered that quickly. Is there something else?"

"There was an issue about a tattoo."

Mark went on to relate a story to Fresher of an incident just after they moved to Hamilton. Kristine was doing most of the coordination for the move as Mark was concentrating on his new Church. About two or three days after they settled in, Kristine got sick, so much so that she was in hospital overnight. The doctor explained that it was a combination of exhaustion and dehydration. When Mark went to pick her up, she was just getting dressed. The sunlight caught her right shoulder and he saw what he thought was the outline of a very faded tattoo that looked like two letters. When asked about it, she just passed it off as a tattoo that she got in university while drunk and had it removed a couple of years later. This year, after the car accident, the attending physician in the hospital who declared her dead came to Mark's room. The doctor extended his condolences. The tattoo came to Mark's mind so he asked the doctor about it. The doctor acknowledged it and explained that there was a marginally successful attempt to have it chemically removed. As is the policy, all body scars and markings must be listed on the physicians report. The tattoo was bleached out but still vivid enough to read, 'AC' under ultra violet light. Mark just assumed that it was an old boyfriend but couldn't help but think that AC was connected to the items in the pouch.

"Mark, is there anything else?"

"Only the photos, but they are just a few memories from French Guiana."

Fresher took the photos out of the envelope and looked at each one, front and back.

"Mark, what are the numbers on the back?"

"I have no idea."

"Mark, where do you want to go with this?"

"Harold, I want you to get to the bottom of all this. I need answers."

"How far? It may get costly."

"The insurance company of the other driver made a sizeable settlement. I want to bring closure not just for me, but for Kristine and her mother. Consider yourself as having a blank cheque."

"I will see what I can do. I need you to do something for me. I would like a recent picture of Kristine, as well as keeping the identification card and ring for a while. Would you please call Kristine's mother and let her know that I will be dropping by to ask a few questions. Let's not alarm her. Tell her I am from the life insurance company and need to have a few routine questions answered before I can complete the claim. Can you also get me the name and number for the sorority sister in Moncton?"

After Mark left the office, Fresher called Samid in.

"Samid, is it my eyes or is there something lightly etched inside this ring?"

"Harold, it looks like there is something. Do you want me to see if I can find out what it is?"

"Yes. I'm off to Regina. I'll call from there."

Chapter 9

Fresher's initial suspicion was that Kristine did, in fact, seek out Mark with a plan to reunite. He also felt there was something more to the time she spent in Montreal. It was almost as if she was trying to disappear after returning from French Guiana. He was hoping deep inside that whatever he found would not be devastating to Mark.

The direct flight from Hamilton to Regina was uneventful. It did give him some time to look at his information a bit more closely and the unanswered questions were piling up. Still the most puzzling and hopefully Samd would be able to help solve the inscription.

Fresher hadn't dressed for the western Canada cool autumn taking only a thin trench coat and was thankful that the cab was warm. Leaving the taxi and feeling the stiff north wind cut at his face, he walked up to Mrs. Locke's front door. Fresher hoped that she was at home and would answer quickly. After one knock, a pleasant looking nicely dressed older woman opened the door. As soon as he mentioned his name, she reached out and took his arm pulling him inside.

"Yes, Dr. Fresher, Mark called and said you would be dropping by. Let me get us some tea."

Within a few minutes, Mrs. Locke returned with a tray of tea and a few biscuits. The tea was exactly what Fresher needed to warm him up.

"Mrs. Locke, first let me express my company's deepest condolences for your loss. It's always difficult losing a family member, especially a child."

"Thank you Dr. Fresher. Yes, I certainly wasn't expecting her death. I just sorted things out from the loss of my husband. I feel so lonely now. Outside of Mark, I have no one left to rely on except for my brother that I have not spoken to in several years. The last I heard from him, he was living on the streets in Vancouver. Oh well, you're not here to listen to my troubles. How can I help you?"

Over the next half an hour, Fresher asked a lot of routine questions that anyone would expect from an insurance company. Was Kristine a sickly young lady? Was she ever hospitalized? Was she vaccinated? Fresher was taking notes.

Fresher then led the discussion to a more personal level.

"Mrs. Locke, in speaking with Reverend Hiott, it seemed to me that they were a very happy couple.

Mrs. Locke took the lead telling Fresher how Mark and Kristine met in high school and she felt that is when they really fell in love. Their reunion and marriage was the highlight of the mother's life. She so wished that her husband lived long enough to see how Kristine turned out.

Fresher then got down to the real questions he wanted answered.

"I understand that Kristine was in French Guiana working for a relief agency."

"Yes. After she graduated, she came home for a week or so, packed and left. She spent a year in French Guiana before coming back to Canada. We were so proud of her for this, but I must admit we were a bit surprised at first when we learned that she was going. We preferred she would settle into a nice job and find a husband. "

"Did she speak of her years at university?"

"Nothing that we didn't already know already. She completed her political science degree at Dalhousie and was involved in a volunteer outreach program in Halifax. She did mention that she was part of a group while at university. I think she called them the Allegorists. I remember asking her what that was and she told us that it just a social group that liked to look at myths and fables."

"When did you see her again?"

"She went right to Montreal after French Guiana. We did have a good chat on the phone and she gave me her contact information. I told her that her father was quite ill but she never made it home until he died in summer of 1976. She lost a lot of weight and her hair was quite short since the last time I saw her. I tried to talk to her about what was going on in her life to make such a physical change but that was the last thing she wanted to talk about. I thought it best to avoid any more discussion on her and focus on her father and the memories. The next time I saw her was when she returned from Montreal in early 1977. What a relief. She told me that she was finished travelling and was going to settle down."

"Did Kristine talk about her work in Montreal?"

"She was fascinated by helping others and went to Montreal to work for an agency for the addicted. I never did get the name. I wish she would have come home more often, but she told me that she was needed there."

"Do you still have the address where she lived in Montreal?"

"Yes. I have it in the drawer. Just a moment. Here it is. Post Office Box 27, Ville Marie, Montreal, Quebec."

"This is a post office box. Do you know where she actually lived?"

"No. She said that she was never at home with her workload. She didn't even have a phone but gave me an emergency number should something happen to her father. We did get the odd letter from here, albeit short letters. I needed to use the emergency number when her father passed away. "

"Did Kristine answer that call you made?"

"No, it was a man, but he must have given her the message quickly as she called me back within an hour."

"Did she ever refer to a friend named Paulette Darion or anyone with the initials AC?"

"No. I don't recall any friends by that name or with those initials. The only person that I knew that she was close to was a young man named Berger. I think his first name was Gils. He came to the funeral with Kristine, but I am not sure how close they were as they stayed in separate bedrooms and I never saw anything between them. She did tell me that he worked with her."

"Gils Berger. He was just a friend?"

"Yes. A mother can tell these things. Besides, he wasn't at all her type. He was fidgety and ate very little."

"Just one last question. Did Kristine ever mention a company called TDM?"

"No."

Mrs. Locke and Fresher spent the next half hour finishing a second cup of tea and Fresher updating her on Mark. She asked the typical questions of a concerned mother-in-law. How was he holding up? Were his injuries healed? Was he back full time to the Ministry?

Fresher responded positively to all her questions leaving Mrs. Locke happy.

****

He spent the return flight digesting what he heard in Regina. Kristine obviously held a passion for helping people. Why did she do this in Montreal under the name Paulette Darion? She was fluent in French so working in Montreal would have been easy. Who is this new character in the mystery, Gils Berger? Could he have been the same man who answered Kristine's mother's call when her father passed away in 1976? Fresher suspected that TDM was the agency both worked for. The mystery included a post office box and an emergency number for Kristine while she was in Montreal. Fresher was now certain; something happened in French Guiana and she was trying to escape or hide.

Fresher returned to Hamilton with more questions than answers.

"Welcome back Harold."

"Thanks Samid. Any luck with the ring?"

"Yes. It's an inscription. *Matthew 7:13 - 21657.*"

"Are you sure?"

"Yes."

Fresher immediately went to his bible to look up what the passage said. *'Enter by the narrow gate. For the gate is wide and the way is easy that leads to destruction, and those who enter by it are many.'* What did this mean and what did numbers 21657 have to do with this?

"Mark, its Harold. I just got back from Regina and your mother-in- law sends her best."

"Did you get any answers?"

"I'm sorry to report that I didn't. I did, however, get a couple of leads that I would like to follow-up on. One is a man by the name of Gils Berger. Did Kristine ever mention him?"

"No, I don't recall that name ever coming up in a conversation. Why?"

"According to Kristine's mother, Berger accompanied Kristine to her father's funeral. I don't think that Berger was a love interest as her mother told me that they stayed in separate bedrooms and were never seen to have anything between them. Mothers have that sense. My guess is that he worked with Kristine in Montreal."

"Anything else?"

"Yes, there is an inscription on the inside of the ring, ' *Matthew 7:13 - 21657'.* "

"I know Matthew 7:13. It's interpreted to mean that taking the easy way out can often lead to destruction, but what are the numbers?"

"I was hoping you could tell me."

"I have no idea."

"21657. A date? An old address? Anything ring a bell?

"No Harold, nothing. Let me write them down and I'll see if I can figure it out. What's your next move?"

I am going to make calls to both Nester Agency and Ann Haggarty. As her sorority sister and boss, she may have some information."

"Harold, I may be able to help you. I know that Ann Haggarty is now in Toronto at Renaissance Development, a funding agency for not-for-profits. She moved from Moncton just before we were married. I found her number in Kristine's address book. If you would like, I could let her know you might be calling."

"That would be appreciated Mark. If I have my dates right, Kristine worked for Ann for only about four to five months.'

"Yes, that would be correct."

"I'll try Nester first and then connect with Haggarty. Not sure what information that I can get, but I don't want to leave anything untouched. Oh, Mark heads up. I may need to go to Montreal for a couple of days. It looks like there may be some answers there. I'll keep you posted."

"Harold, I can't thank you enough. I feel that some of the weight of this has been lifted off my shoulders already. Good luck."

Back in his office, he looked over a few messages on his desk before putting them down and refocusing. "Samid, can you get me the numbers for the Nester Agency in Moncton and Renaissance Development in Toronto? Also, see if you can make any sense of the numbers in the ring."

Fifteen minutes later Fresher picked up the phone and called the Nester Agency in Moncton. After a short wait, he was transferred to the Gail LeBlanc, Executive Director. He explained that he was representing Mark in trying to answer some questions regarding Kristine that Mark. Ms LeBlanc remembered both Mark and Kristine very well. She heard about the accident through some of the folks in the community and offered her condolences. She recalled Kristine as a hard working outreach worker who was very well liked by all. She was particularly good with the French speaking clients as she spoke proficiently. They were all sad to see her leave but they understood the life of a Minister's wife and knew that one day they could move on.

"Ms LeBlanc, does the name Gils Berger or the letters AC mean anything to you?"

"No. I do not recall anyone on staff with that name or those initials."

"Do the numbers 21657 mean anything to you?"

"No, can't say that I recall those numbers."

Fresher thanked Ms LeBlanc and hung up. Great, he thought, no answers.

The next call was more rewarding. "Hello, Ms Haggarty? My name is Harold Fresher. Do you have a few minutes?"

"Hello Dr. Fresher. Please call me Ann. Mark Hiott called and told me to expect you. I felt so sorry that I could not attend Kristine's funeral but I was in the States on business. What a loss. Kristine was one of a kind. What can I help you with?"

"I understand that you hired Kristine in Moncton."

"Yes, I did."

"Can you tell me about her?"

Ann Haggarty went on to provide the information she remembered. It included meeting Kristine at Dalhousie's frosh week 1969. They were in many of the same classes and enjoyed similar campus activities, one of which was volunteering for an outreach program targeting the under-housed and homeless in the north end of Halifax, a poor part of town. Kristine took Haggarty on her missions a few times. She knew that Kristine was very well liked by the outreach agency and seemed to have a knack of dealing with people in a compassionate and supportive manner. Kristine even received a community award for her work. When they graduated in spring of 1972, Kristine went off on an international aid program. There were all kinds of these recruitment posters on campus.

"Ann you said that you enjoyed similar campus activities. Were there others besides the outreach program?"

"Yes. We both played inter-mural volleyball, and were members of the Allegorists. Before you ask me what that was, it was a group of students who were interested in myths, their origin, their meaning, their position today, etc. We were always looking at the strange things throughout history. A good example would be, 'myth of Ham'. It examines black and white Americans' recourse to the biblical character of Ham as a cultural strategy for explaining racial origins. I must admit that I saw Allegorists as a vacation for my mind away from the studying. Kristine, however, was really into it compared to others."

"What do you mean, 'really into it'? "

"She kept every note, researched every name and myth, and kept as much information as she could get. Like I said, she was really into it. "

"When did you hear from her after university?"

"July 1977."

"July 1977?"

"Yes, that was the first time I heard from her since graduation. She called me from Regina and asked me if the Nester agency had any jobs that might be suitable for her. I requested she fax me a resume which looked good, and therefore with the agency growing, especially in the French community, I offered her a job, but made it clear that we couldn't pay for the move from Regina."

"Let me restate, she called you for a job?"

""Yes. It was right out of the blue."

Fresher tucked that in his memory. Mark told him that Haggarty called Kristine, but that was not so and this wasn't something that Mark would have gotten wrong.

"Did her resume mention what she was doing from 1972 to 1977?"

"Well, you have to keep in mind that information on a resume is confidential. But, I guess it would be okay now that she is gone. As I remember, Kristine did go on an international aid program to French Guiana right after university but returned in mid 1972. She went to Montreal and worked for TDM, Toxicomanie Du Montreal. I know from my connections in the industry that they are a well revered agency in Montreal that deals with outreach to drug addiction."

Fresher thought to himeself - TDM - Toxicomanie Du Montreal. Finally an answer. He made a mental note to connect with them.

"Do you know Paulette Darion, Gils Berger or recognize the initials AC?"

"No, I don't recall ever meeting people by those names. The initials are vaguely familiar but in my line of work, everything has a short form."

"Do the numbers 21657 mean anything to you?"

"21657, no I can't say I know what they stand for."

"Ann, you have been very helpful. Is there anything else that you can tell me?"

"Dr. Fresher, I knew that Kristine was in love with Mark. The few months I was in Moncton prior to the wedding, we often talked. Yes, Kristine was truly in love. She kept telling me that her life was complete."

"Thankyou Ann."

Chapter 10

Fresher sat in his office reflecting on the information he gathered. He made a quick call to Mark to let him know that he was going to Halifax before Montreal. He explained that a student interest group at Dalhousie named the Allegorists came up in a conversation with not just him, but also Mrs. Locke as well as Ann Haggarty. He wanted to get first hand information and also needed to make sure that he still had a blank cheque for this case.

The flight from Hamilton to Halifax was a bit rocky given that it was nearing late October when gusty east winds began to dominate the autumn weather. He took a taxi directly from the airport to Dalhousie University. His first stop was the Administration office where he introduced himself to the receptionist as Dr. Harold Fresher. This is where his PhD would come in handy. It was an impressive title and gave him a level of credibility that made it easy for people to comply with his requests. He asked to speak with the Director of Administration.

The receptionist picked up the phone, made a short quiet remark and within less than a minute, a man emerged from an office from behind the receptionist.

"Dr. Fresher, my name is Dr. Chad Elliot. I am the Director of Administration here at Dalhousie. Please come in and have a seat. What can I help you with?"

Fresher smiled to himself as Elliot stressed the word doctor. He was obviously very precise and oozed the stuffiness of the old ivy halls.

Fresher went on to tell Elliot that one of Dalhousie's alumni was killed in a car accident earlier this year. Her name while a student was Kristine Locke and she graduated in 1972 with a political science degree and was active in inter-mural volleyball as well as part of a club called the Allegorists. She also volunteered for an outreach program and received a community award for her work. Fresher explained that he was asked by her husband, Rev. Mark Hiott in Hamilton to look into some of her history. Her husband was grieving and needed to fill in some of the gaps in her life.

"Dr. Fresher, we usually do not provide any details of our students, however, you say she died. Are there any of our alumni or teaching staff who can confirm this?"

"Yes. I believe that if you call Ann Haggarty, class of 1972, she will confirm. Here is her number in Toronto. Please give her a call and I will come back this afternoon."

That afternoon, Dr. Elliot confirmed what Fresher knew and provided more information that Fresher hoped for. In very precise language, Elliot interpreted Kristine's file relating that she was an average student who graduated with a political science degree in 1972. She optioned French as a minor for two years. Her inter-mural activities included volley ball and a club called the Allegorists. She was commended for her work with an outreach agency and was a member of a sorority. Fresher sat listening as if Elliot was playing back a recording of what Fresher said earlier that day. Fresher thought with an inward smile, this was so typical of a university, - an academic like Elliot in charge of administration.

"I was wondering if there was a student at that time by the name of Gils Berger."

"Let me look. We had a George Burger in the 50's but no Gils Berger on file."

"Is there any chance that the teaching supervisor for the Allegorists is still on staff?"

"Yes, it's Brent Roberts and he still leads the group. As a matter in fact, he should be in Killan library right now preparing for his group later this afternoon."

Fresher walked the short distance to the library. "Mr. Roberts, I am Dr. Harold Fresher. Dr. Elliot at Admin told me that I could find you here. I was wondering if I could have a few minutes of your time.

"Yes, Chad called and said you were coming over."

Mr. Roberts, I wasn't sure if you knew that one of your students, Kristine Locke was killed earlier this year."

"I just found out from Chad. That's such a shame. Kristine was one of the best the club ever included. Chad also said that she was married to a Minister. That's quite unexpected."

"Why unexpected?"

"Kristine was very much involved with helping the homeless, but her attraction to myths was far greater. I wasn't surprised that she went to French Guiana as soon as she graduated. Chasing myths and marrying Ministers don't really go together. "

"Mr. Roberts, her husband, Rev. Mark Hiott has asked me to look into Kristine's background. He feels there is so much he didn't know. I was hoping you could help."

Over the next several minutes, Roberts opened up and there was no denying that the Allegorists group was quite special to him. He recalled every student, every myth, and every outcome. Kristine was one of his more memorable students. Over the three years in the group, she was the most vocal, the most inquisitive, and the one who he felt might go on to investigating myths. He even recalled a session that took the group through the myths of Andre Clousiot. Clousiot was an inmate at Saint-Laurent du-Maroni in French Guiana the same time that the infamous Henri Charriere, better known as Papillion was there. Charriere received the bulk of the modern day notoriety because he wrote a book about his experiences. The truth was that Clousiot was much more celebrated in French Guiana than Papillion. The myths of Clousiot's several escapes and his continual captures are known by every man woman and child in the country. Each escape and each capture was embellished over the years and he became almost a national hero in French Guiana. Legend was that there were between five and seven escapes from Saint-Laurent du-Maroni before his eventual incarceration at Devil's Island. Kristine became engrossed in the myth of the multiple escapes and captures, seeking out the details behind each one. The stories of the intolerable conditions, the bribery, the swamps, and the torture - it was all fodder for Kristine's imagination.

"Mr. Roberts, did you say Andre Clousiot?"

"Yes, Dr. Fresher. There is quite a world-wide interest in this character. I know that a few of the followers consider themselves part of the 'AC Society.'

Bingo, thought Fresher; the tattoo - AC for Andre Clousiot. This must the answer to a major part of the mystery he thought, especially since Kristine tried to have it removed.

Roberts went on to tell Fresher that Kristine's adventure to French Guiana was to pursue the myths surrounding Clousiot. In fact, he received a card from Kristine while she was there. She wrote that she was having a wonderful time and met others who were keenly interested in Clousiot, including a chap named Gils Berger from Quebec City.

"Did you have any contact with her after she returned to Canada?"

"No. The only time I heard from her was a post card from Cayenne."

Fresher left the university very excited. He not only uncovered the meaning of the AC tattoo, but also that she linked up with Berger in French Guiana. Fresher knew that he must now go to Montreal where he hoped he could connect more dots.

****

Fresher considered taking the train from Halifax to Montreal to save Mark a few dollars but the ride would be over twenty four hours. He decided to stay overnight in Halifax and take an early morning flight to Montral. The flight gave him time to crystalizing his findings. Things were slowly coming together. The AC tatoo conection to Clousiot, meeting Berger in French Guiana but still the nagging issues surrounding her time in Montreal especially why she took an alias and why so secretive about her address. His theory was getting traction; she was running from something that happened in French Guiana, and yes, she purposely tracked Mark down and led an exemplary life while reunited with him. He was finally getting more answers than questions.

The plane landed late morning. As soon as he deboarded, he walked to a bank of payphones. Toxicomanie Du Montreal wasn't hard to find. It was in the phone book with an address on Marcel Street, Montreal. A short taxi ride took him to noticeably a very poor part of town. Fresher looked at the outside of the building and wondered if there was anyone working in the place. The building was in poor condition with graffiti on every exterior wall. A small sign above the door read, ' Toxicomanie Du Montreal.' There were three young people sleeping on the sidewalk a few feet from the door under a single dim light shining from a window of the building. He entered the door and the inside was a reflection of the outside. The floors were dirty, the counter badly damaged, a few mismatched desks and chairs, a wall of old filing cabintes, and a long table with an assortment of warm juices, drying fruits, and blankets piled on top. No one was in sight. Was this the agency that Haggarty said was so well revered? Fresher heard the tolet flush in the back of the large room. Out came a middle aged man with long dirty hair, an old sweater and pants and an unshaven face. He looked startled seeing Fresher standing in a suit with a topcoat.

"Monseur, Puis-je t'aider?"

"Do you speak English."

"Yes. Can I help you?"

Fresher was guarded with his words except to say that he was looking for information about Paulette Dorion. He showed the man the ID card with Kristine's picture on it. He related that she died in an accident and he was in Montreal to finalize the life insurance claim. He went on to tell the man that she could have worked there anytime from 1973 to 1977.

Unfortunately, the man had no recollection. He wasn't on staff, he was a volunteer. The TDM Manager would be back in an hour and he was welcome to wait. He was also welcome to a coffee, but one look at the pot and Fresher wasn't interested.

Fifteen minutes later the Manager arrived. "Monseur, Puis-je t'aider?"

"Do you speak English."

"Yes. I am told that you are looking for information about an old employee. A Paulette Darion, around 1973 to 1977?"

"Yes. Fresher repeated what he told the volunteer. He showed the TDM Manager the ID card with her picture on it and explained that she died in an accident and he was in Montreal on behalf of the insurance company.

"What would youlike to know?"

Fresher was able to learn that Kristine worked for TDM for over three and a half years. She was hired at the same time as a man called Serge Piche. Piche was on volunteer assignment with Kristine in French Guiana and neighbouring Suriname. Both offered solid resumes in outreach programming, and both spoke French and English which was a requirement at TDM. The resumes were not checked completely as it was very difficult to confirm any international work quickly. TDM took a leap of faith on them and gave them work, but only twenty hours each per week. They both did a wonderful job while there were there. The two seemed quite close, but people knew they were just friends even though they apparently shared an apartment. Tragically, Piche was gunned down outside of a bar in April 1977. The real revelation for the TDM Manager was that newspapers exposed Serge Piche as really a man called Gils Berger, from Quebec City.

"Did you say Gils Berger was this Serge Piche?"

"Yes."

The Manager went on to tell Fresher that within a day of the shooting, Paulette left suddenly. There was no resignation letter or a forwarding address. He went on to explain that in the not-for-profit world, staff come and go, sometimes quickly. The outreach folks get their fill of seeing the human disaster on the streets and give up, and in some cases, actually become one of the clients.

"Whatever the reason people leaving, we accept it and move on. There are lots of folks wanting to help just waiting for their opportunity."

"Would there be any other employees who might have worked with Paulette and Serge?"

"Besides me, there is one person who was here during that time, but she is on vacation for another week and a half."

"Would you have a picture of Piche?"

"No, I am afraid not. We destroy our files after seven years."

"One last question if you don't mind. Do the numbers 21657 mean anything?"

"Is it an address?"

"I don't know."

"I'm afraid not."

"Thank you

Fresher wasn't sure what to do next, so he found a local bistro and enjoyed lunch. As he finished, he pieced together what he heard. Gils Berger used the Piche alias only in Montreal as Kristine's mother mentioned Berger attending the father's funeral. Berger, alias Piche was gunned down in front of a bar and Kristine suddenly left. Judging by the dates, she dropped the alias Paulette Darion and went home to Regina right after the shooting. It was getting much clearer that both Kristine and Berger were hiding something that happened in French Guiana.

That afternoon, Fresher found the address of the apartment that he received from the TDM Manager.

1228 St. Denis Street was a very old building built in the 1930's. Fresher wasn't surprised that the lock on the door into the building was broken as the entire neighbourhood once experienced better days. Apartment 7 was on the second floor. No elevator and the stairs creaked badly. Fresher got to the door of the apartment and knocked lightly. A young lady opened the door as far as the safety chain would allow.

"Sorry to disturb you, but I am looking for Paulette Darion. I understand that she was an occupant around 1975. Here is a picture of her. I was wondering if you knew her."

The young lady spoke in broken English and made enough sense to let Fresher know that they took over the apartment only a few months ago after an old man moved to a long term care home. She did not recognize the picture or the name. The woman closed the door abruptly leaving Fresher staring at his hand holding the picture.

On his way down the stairs, he saw a sign on a first floor apartment. It read 'Surintendant'. No harm in trying he thought. An older man came to the door. The dirty tank top matched the four day old stubble on his face and even though it was well before noon, a very clear odor of beer was on his breath. With a cigarette in hand, he looked at Fresher and said, "You a cop?"

"No, sir, I am not. I was looking for old friends of mine, Paulette Darion and Serge Piche."

"I'm surprised they had any friends. Damned couple, they were. They were always fighting about something. Didn't surprise me Piche was shot a few years ago. The day before he was gunned down I could hear the yelling.

"Do you know what it was about?"

"Piche was into selling drugs and she wanted no part of it. Everyone knew it, even the police. After he was shot, they came by and searched the place. That's the last I heard about anything. The dame flew the coop. They owed me two hundred dollars. You here to pay me?"

"No, I'm just trying to get some answers."

Before Fresher could ask any more questions, the man slammed the door.

As Fresher left the building, he was convinced that French Guiana created a situation for Kristine that prevented her from returning to a more comfortable life in Regina rather than living in this place. What he couldn't understand was why her companion got into drugs and shot dead.

His next stop was the Urbain, one of the many local newspapers. The Urbain was a tabloid that always looked for the sensational stories. He was hoping for some information on the shooting.

Fresher didn't have any command of the French language, but knew the date, April 1977, and the fact that Berger was shot down in front of a bar. Starting with April

1, 1977 he brought up the front pages of the paper and didn't need to go too far. Friday April 9, headline - Meurtre - murder. He took a copy to the clerk and asked if there was anyone who could translate the article for him.

"Monsieur, we have a translation service. We charge by the hour. This article should take about two hours but we have a few jobs ahead of yours. Can you come back after tomorrow around 10:00?"

It had been a long time since he had an entire evening to sit back and relax. After an early dinner, he took on a showing of Dangerous Liaisons at the Montreal Theatre. As he got comfortable in his seat, he chuckled that Kristine Locke could have been the subject of the play.

At 10:00 sharp the next morning, Fresher returned to the Urbain and collected the translated story. The original article was only a quarter page of the tabloid, but did provide some additional information. The tabloid reported that the police were called to a local bar, the Faucon doré, late Friday evening where 31 year old Gils Berger, using the alias Serge Piche was found shot to death. Berger, a native of Quebec City was working for Toxicomanie Du Montreal, an outreach agency. Police suspected that Berger was caught up in a drug deal that went bad as a few days prior to his death he was arrested in a roundup of drug dealers but released for lack of evidence. The rest of the article was not directly related to the shooting or drugs, but more on Berger's background in Quebec City including a brief volunteer stint in French Guiana.

Chapter 11

As long as he was in Montreal, he thought that he would look into the shooting in front of the bar. The taxi ride to Faucon doré was almost a half an hour as the traffic was heavier than usual. It was a typical sleazy corner bar where the tables hadn't been wiped since they were installed. The repaired chairs and new patches of unpainted drywall were evidence of a bar fight or two. The smell of cigarette smoke and stale beer clung to everything inside. Fresher made a mental note to have his coat dry cleaned as soon as he could. A few neon lights helped customers to see the bar and the sign that pointed to the washrooms.

It was too early for the after-work customers so there was nobody at the tables. Fresher's eyes adjusted to the dingy atmosphere seeing only one man nursing a small draft beer at the far end of the bar and staring at a television that was chained to the wall.

"Puis-je pou vous? said a man behind the bar without even looking up.

"Anglais?"

'What can I get you?"

"I am looking for some information."

The bartender looked up with a cold stare. "You the police?"

"No. The ten dollar bill that Fresher slid across the counter was quickly picked up.

"I am trying to get some information about a woman who died in an accident a few months ago in Hamilton, Ontario. We do know that she lived in Montreal, St. Denis Street, for a few years. This is an ID picture of her. Do you know her?"

Almost before Fresher finished his sentence, the bartender said no.

Fresher dropped a twenty dollar bill on the bar and continued. "She was friends with a man, Gils Berger. He was shot outside your front door April 9, 1977. He used the alias Serge Piche. I was wondering if that would refresh your memory."

"Just why are you so interested?"

"It's an insurance matter."

"Monsieur, I recall quite well that shooting. It closed my business for a few days and it took a long time for many of the regulars to come back. Piche, or Berger, or whatever name he used, was bad news. He got into selling drugs before he was shot and I heard after the shooting that he was skimming some of the money. His suppliers didn't take kindly to this and those guys have no tolerance for losing money. That's all I know."

It was clear to Fresher that the bartender wasn't enjoying the conversation.

"Have another look at the picture. Can you tell me anything about her?"

"Look pal, if this broad was connected to that druggie, I hope she's long gone"

"Well, I appreciate your time."

As Fresher was leaving, he passed the corridor to the washroom. On both walls were several photographs, couples and group of people surrounded by Christmas decorations.

Fresher walked back to the bar. "I see a whole bunch of pictures on the wall over there. What are they?"

"We have a New Years Eve party every year. I give folks the Polaroid camera and they take pictures of themselves and put it up on the wall. We started this in 1972 and have over sixteen years worth of memories. Have a look if you want. The left hand side is the start."

Fresher went over to one of the photo walls and zeroed in on 1974, 1975, and 1976. There in 1976 was a picture of Kristine with a man beside her who had his arm on her shoulder. On his arm was a tattoo, 'AC' and on her right index finger was the eight sided ring. He took the picture off the wall and went back to the bar.

"Do you know the man in this picture?"

"I forgot all about that picture. That's Piche, or Berger, whatever you call him."

"Do you know the girl he is with?"

"She would come in with him every so often. I don't remember her name, and I don't recall seeing her after the shooting. Hey, isn't that the same girl in the ID photo you showed me?"

"Can I have this picture?" He slipped the barman another ten dollar bill.

"Sure."

Fresher now owned a picture of Berger.

"One last question if you don't mind. Did Piche chum with anyone?"

"No. The odd time he and the broad would sit with the pawnbroker."

"The pawnbroker?"

"Yes, he sat with Piche and the girl in the booth over in the corner a few times. They were quiet and never had more than one beer each. I remember they were lousy tippers. Now that I think of it, once Piche got into the drug business, I didn't see the pawnbroker anymore."

"Where is this pawnbroker?"

"Five or six doors down the street."

****

As soon as Fresher got outside, he looked up and down the street and the pawn shop was not hard to find. There was and old metal sign hanging out over the sidewalk. As Fresher approached he could see that the windows and door were equipped with more bars than a bird cage. Behind the heavy glass was the usual array of pawned items in the windows - watches, cameras, jewellery and a belt buckle. Fresher smiled wondering why a pawnbroker would take in and display a dull finished round belt buckle with an arrow pointing out sideways. The sign beside it said eight dollars and by the look of the dust, it had been there for some time.

As Fresher opened the door, he heard a buzzer go off, an alert for any customer entering. He walked in slowly and saw a middle aged, heavy set man behind a Plexi-glass enclosure with a six inch opening across the bottom. He stared at Fresher but said nothing. Fresher saw that his hands were under the counter, probably holding a handgun or rifle.

"Hello, my name is Dr. Harold Fresher." He hoped that pulling out the doctor card would lighten the mood.

"Is someone sick?"

"No. I'm a private investigator."

"So, healing people isn't lucrative enough?'

"No, I'm not that kind of doctor."

"What brings you here?"

Fresher proceeded to tell the pawnbroker that a woman was killed in Hamilton, Ontario a few months ago and he was trying to piece together some events for her husband. He knew that she lived in Montreal for a couple of years.

"The bartender down the street told me that you drank with her and her friend at the bar a couple of times. Would you have a look at this picture?"

Fresher took out the picture from the bar wall and slid it under the glass. The pawnbroker glanced as it quickly but never picked it up. With a smirk on his face, the pawnbroker acknowledged that he knew them both.

"That's Paulette Darion and Serge Piche. I guess you already know that Piche's real name is Berger."

"How well did you know them?"

"I've got nothing to tell you." He waved Fresher out of the shop.

Fresher slowly reached in his pocket and pulled out a twenty dollar bill and laid it on the counter. The pawnbroker scooped up the money.

"Really, you a cop?"

"No. As I said, I am here to help a friend out, nothing more and nothing less."

"You said you were a doctor. What kind?"

Fresher briefly told him about his PhD and that his office was in Hamilton. He was a licensed investigator and he showed him his ID card. Anything that the pawnbroker told him would be the strictest confidence.

"Information costs."

Fresher slipped another twenty dollar bill under the opening.

The pawnbroker picked up the money. "What do you want to know?"

"First, let me tell you what I know. Maybe it will help. In a nutshell, I think that these two were running from something, perhaps something that happened outside of Canada. They both changed their name when they returned to Canada. I know Piche got into the drug business only a few months before he was shot. The work they did was not high paying, so that might explain why he needed to get into the drug business, but why didn't he do this as soon as he got to Montreal is a mystery."

The pawnbroker stared long and hard at Fresher. "For another hundred, I think I can help you with your mystery."

Fresher laid out five more twenties that were quickly taken.

"Grab a chair Doc. You'll enjoy this. Where do you want me to start?"

"The beginning."

The pawnbroker's story was way beyond anything Fresher suspected. He first met Piche in September 1973. Piche and Darion came into his store asking if they could sell a rough diamond. Diamonds were often pried from their settings and sold but each had a jeweller's mark and the pawnbroker had already been fined for pawning stolen gems. He took a closer look at the stone and immediately realized that it was very rough and unpolished but with some value. No one ever stole uncut diamonds so he didn't ask questions and purchased the singular diamond. He told Fresher that in his trade, there is often what he called a calculated risk but Piche and Darion looked and acted too naive to cause him much concern. He took the diamond to a jeweller who he could trust and it turned out that the diamond was an alluvial diamond, found mostly in the volcanic fields of South America. They don't have the same commercial value as a regular diamond, but were worth something if purchased cheaply, cut, polished and sold. He continued to purchase single diamonds from Piche and Darion for almost three years, and sell them to the jeweller. After not seeing the pair for about two months, he bumped into them at the bar and they told him that there were no more diamonds.

"I recall that day very well. See the ring on the girl's finger in the picture? Piche wanted her to take it off and pawn it but she said made a big deal saying no, got up and left."

The pawnbroker went on to tell Fresher that he suspected that the reason Piche turned to the drug business was to compensate for the diamonds being all gone. It wasn't more than a few weeks after their last meeting that Piche was gunned down.

"How many diamonds were there?"

"Sixteen in total."

"One last question. Do the numbers 21657 mean anything to you?"

"Nope. All my pawn tickets start with a letter."

Fresher thanked the pawnbroker and turned to leave when he stopped and turned around.

"How much do you want for the belt buckle in the window?"

The pawnbroker laughed. "I've had that think for two years and not a nibble of interest. Take it, it's yours."

****

Fresher sat on the evening plane from Montreal to Hamilton with a story that was something out of a novel. He now had something substantial for Mark. What Mark wanted to do with it was up to him.

Back in his office the next morning, Fresher was welcomed by Samid with a fresh cup of Sumatra coffee and messages.

"Samid, I notice that you like those wide belts. I bought you back a gift from my travels"

Samid opened the bag and pulled out the belt buckle. He broke out in a huge smile. "This is wonderful; so unique and I really like unique. Thank you Harold." With that, Samid almost danced out of the office.

Fresher sipped his coffee as he called Mark and asked him to meet that night over dinner. He told him to make it early as there was a lot of information for Mark to digest.

Chapter 12

It was October twenty sixth and the restaurant was decorated for Halloween. As promised by Fresher, dinner was a two hour affair. Fresher started at the beginning laying out every detail that he gathered to date with Mark not interrupting once. He told Mark that he was sure Kristine studied French in university not to work in Canada but to use it in French Guiana. That trip was to follow the myth of Clousiot, a prisoner that she developed a keen interest in. Apparently, Clousiot became a bit of a cult hero in French Guiana where he served time in the Saint-Laurent du-Maroni prison. He escaped and was recaptured many times and the stories were so embellished that the myth only got bigger. Kristine's tattoo, AC, was recognition that she was part of the Andre Clousiot Society. She did meet a man while in French Guiana, a volunteer from Quebec City by the name of Gils Berger. Both were chasing the AC myth. By now Mark was sitting very erect in his chair with his eyes glued on Fresher listening to how they left French Guiana and went to Montreal where they both worked for Toxicomanie Du Montreal, also known as TDM, a local not-for-profit outreach agency. That is when they took alias'. Gils Berger became Serge Piche and Kristine became Paulette Darion.

"Mark, here is where things get interesting. They changed their names because they smuggled diamonds back from French Guiana and there must have been some concern that they would be followed."

Mark's face went pale. "Harold, diamonds; smuggling diamonds?"

Fresher explained that they sold rough diamonds to a pawnbroker in Montreal. They were alluvial diamonds that were indigenous to South America. They lived off the proceeds for a few years because they were both part time employees. The diamonds ran out and when they were all gone, Berger turned to drugs. Fresher assured Mark that he was convinced through his investigation that Kristine was not into drugs.

He also confirmed that they shared an apartment probably to keep an eye on each other regarding the diamonds. From what friends said about the two, they weren't a couple but just friends. He repeated from an earlier conversation that Berger accompanied her from Montreal to Regina for her father's funeral and that Kristine's mother she saw nothing between her daughter and Berger. They used their real names on the trip to Regina, no doubt to not alarm family and friends and to make travel easier.

The New Year's photo Fresher found at a local bar was brought out. Fresher pointed out that the man with Kristine was Berger, both with the same tattoo, and she was wearing the ring. Fresher put the ring on the table and re-read the inscription. *Matthew 7:13 – 21657*

"Harold, as I said, I know this passage very well. 'Enter by the narrow gate. For the gate is wide and the way is easy that leads to destruction, and those who enter by it are many,'."

"Is there anything else about the passage?"

"Well, it could have a number of meanings but Matthew was also known as Levi."

"Mark, this is confusing enough. Any more thought about the numbers?"

"No. I tried every biblical connection and I found nothing."

"Harold, what about this Berger fellow?"

"He was shot and killed. The police suspected that it was drug related. As I mentioned, the drug business developed after they ran out of the diamonds but Kristine was not happy about it. Their landlord heard arguments, the gist of which was Kristine yelling at Berger to get out of the drug business. It looks like Kristine fled Montreal for Regina right after the shooting.

"Harold, I feel numb. Is there anything more to this?"

"Something that might answer your suspicion about Kristine finding you. Kristine didn't get a call from Haggarty regarding a job in Moncton. Kristine called Ann for a job."

Mark sat totally deflated.

"Mark, I've exhausted Kristine's friends, Dalhousie, her activities and time in Montreal. I believe that the reference she made in her letter to you, *'There was, however, a period in my life that could have been better. It was between the end of university and my arrival in Moncton'* was about the diamonds and Montreal. I think we know about Montreal, and less about French Guiana. I will keep trying to unlock the ring code, but I am not sure I can do much else without going to French Guiana and looking for something."

"Harold, you have gone too far to give up now. Give me a call when you get back."

"Mark, are you sure? I could be chasing a myth, pardon the expression. It could lead to nothing."

"Harold, we have come this far, so what could be worse, not trying or not trying harder?"

As the men were leaving the restaurant, three women from Mark's congregation were coming in. Fresher remembered seeing them at coffee hour, especially the middle aged brunette. She was what men would call attractive for her age. Mark introduced the ladies to Fresher. Fresher shook their hands holding onto Jenn Gallager's hand a little longer. Mark smiled slightly seeing a connection between the two.

****

The next morning, back in his office, he asked Samid to clear his calendar for the next week and arrange for return flights to Cayenne in French Guiana and find a hotel while he was there.

"Samid, book the least expensive flights."

"Harold, you do know that it's the middle of summer in French Guiana, don't you?"

"Probably hot."

"Hot will be the cool part of the day."

Chapter 13

The flight to Cayenne Airport in French Guiana was a two leg trip, stopping in Caracas Venezuela to change flights. Fresher knew that Samid could have booked an Air France flight direct to Cayenne, but he was trying to save Mark money.

The first leg was five hours, just long enough to be uncomfortable. He made a note to see how much an upgrade would be for the return trip. The layover in Caracas was scheduled to be less than three hours so he didn't really have a lot of time once he ate lunch in the airport. He was never on South American soil so he decided to take a short stroll outside. It was very short. The temperature was just over one hundred and the humidity extremely high. Samid was right. Within minutes, he was soaked to the point that he went back inside and went to the washroom to change his shirt. Fortunately, everything was in one carryon bag for what he expected to be a short trip.

He soon found out that flying a regional carrier on the second leg to Cayenne was beyond an interesting experience. The plane was a twenty seat bush craft less than half full. There were ten seats on each side of the narrow aircraft and no seat assignments so Fresher took a seat mid plane. The seats in front, behind and across the aisle were empty. What a relief he thought but that relief was short lived as a Creole woman boarded the plane and sat in the empty seat to his left dropping a crate of chickens in the aisle between Fresher and the woman. With no air conditioning on the plane, the combination of body odour and chicken droppings was intolerable. Fresher moved to a seat a few rows ahead. As soon as the plane took off, the seat in front of him, occupied by an older plump man, dropped back. It was broken. It was a long, unbearable forty minute flight.

As the plane was nearing its destination, Fresher looked out the window and recognized the jungle, rivers and hills from the photos Mrs. Locke sent back to Mark. He couldn't help but think that it would be very easy to get lost in this land.

The coastal town of Cayenne was torrid, even hotter than Samid implied. A wall of humid heat almost pushed him back as he exited the terminal. Fortunately, a couple of taxis were parked outside and immediately Fresher jumped inside the closest vehicle handing the driver a note with the hotel name on it. The taxi was a Pontiac at least twenty years old and the only air conditioning was the open window. Within half a mile, Fresher was soaked. The ride to L'Hotel du Manoire on La Rocade did, however, allow him to see some of the city. It was a mix of old world architecture dotted by a few modern structures. Most of the buildings were white with a coloured tiled roof. There was a combination of cars, bikes, and horse and oxen pulled carts, all sharing the road. The vegetation was lush deep green with several varieties of bright flowers. He was able to understand the driver's broken English along the way who told him that it was a good time to be visiting as the wet season was a month away and it rained every day for over two months.

"Does it get any cooler at night?"

The driver broke out laughing. "Non Monsieur."

Samid booked accommodation off the beaten track. The two star hotel was an older grey block building with a red clay roof. Large letters were painted in the outer wall, L'Hotel du Manoire. There was no glass in the main floor windows, only open storm shutters that were well used. After paying the driver, Fresher walked inside to see a clean and nicely maintained lobby. The open area was cooled by two large ceiling fans rotating slowly. Just inside the door was an old wooden check-in desk with room keys hanging on the wall. On the far side of a large lobby was a six stool bar with four small tables close by. The place gave Fresher the feeling that he was in Rick's Bar in Casablanca but without the piano. The bartender was busy hand drying glasses and looked like he tended the bar for a few decades. There was a kitchen off to the side sending out a very tempting spicy aroma. His mouth watered. He planned to try the food that evening.

A woman behind the desk smiled at him and motioned him over.

In very good English she said, "You must be Dr. Fresher."

"Yes, how did you know?"

"We only have one reservation for tonight. I can give you a room with a shared lavatory, or our executive room with private bathroom. It's an additional three dollars US."

"The executive please."

"Good. Please sign in and I'll give you your key."

His room was one of three on the second floor. Of course there was no elevator, but there was a window air conditioning unit running full blast blowing tepid air. No question that his definition of executive was far different that the woman at the desk. It didn't matter. He was there only a couple of days and all he needed was a bed and a place to clean up.

Feeling refreshed after a luke warm shower, he put on shorts, a golf shirt and running shoes. By the time he walked down the flight of stairs to the lobby, he could feel drops of sweat on his forehead. He made a direct path for the bar.

"Beer?" the bartender said in excellent English.

"Yes please."

"Glass?"

"No, bottle is good, thanks."

"You must be Canadian."

"How did you know?"

"You're polite. Here you go, our finest local brew."

The first sip was wonderful. The second sip seemed to finally slow down the feeling of the heat.

He found out that the chatty bartender was a transplanted Californian who moved to this country twenty three years ago. His goal was to be a prospector but wound up meeting the daughter of the hotel owner and getting married. They decided to buy the hotel from her father and make their fortune in tourism. It wasn't long before he spoke French fluently and his wife, the woman at the check-in was already bilingual. They never made their fortune, but were happy.

A couple of the tables were now occupied, one by a pair of Italian speaking student tourists judging by their boots and back packs, and an older couple who were speaking French and enjoying a drink. Probably locals, he thought.

"This beer is excellent and I smell something cooking."

"It's the daily special, in fact all we serve is a daily special. Today it was the spicy curry stew with fresh warm flat bread."

"Perfect. Can I have an order please?"

"You Canadians, no end to the politeness."

The bartender went to the kitchen and returned in less than a minute with Fresher's dinner. It was exactly what Fresher hoped for, and with the beer would be one of those meals that one doesn't easily forget. He was reminded something his father told him many years before. 'A meal is memorable for both the food and the circumstance'.

As he was finishing his dinner, the bartender asked him what brought Fresher to French Guiana. Fresher ordered another beer and explained he was there on behalf of a friend in Canada who lost his wife and wanted to understand to some unanswered questions about his wife's youth. She came here to volunteer for an agency in May 1972 and her husband was interested in the work she did.

"You must be a good friend to travel all this way looking for a few answers."

Fresher was careful not to mention his role as a private investigator. He knew that word in these towns can travel fast and may stifle responses to his questions.

"Yes good friends. Perhaps you can tell me where the agency offices are."

"There is only one office. It acts as the unified international relief agency office in French Guiana. It's about a ten minute walk away. They are closed now but tomorrow morning, just turn right outside the front door and you won't miss it.'

"Thanks. Tell me. Have you heard of the Andre Clousiot Society?"

The bartender let out a laugh. "Yes, who hasn't, why the interest?"

"My friend's wife wore an AC tattoo on her and I understand that this may be the membership card for the Society."

The next half hour was taken by the bartender telling Fresher about Andre Clousiot and the Society. To the bartender, those folks were chasing rainbows. French Guiana was full of tales and myths, largely about prisoners who were jailed in either Saint-Laurent du Maroni prison or on Devil's Island. Of course, Henri Charriere, better known as Papillion was the most famous because he wrote a book, but Clousiot was the one who supposedly made so many escapes and was recaptured. Fresher also found out that Devil's Island was not really a prison, rather an internment camp and escape was an impossibility given the rough waters, under current and rocks. The real prison was at Saint-Laurent du Maroni where Clousiot was kept.

The bartender went on to tell Fresher that an old man living in a small village near Cottica, a town one hundred and thirty miles west of Cayenne near the French Guiana – Suriname. Cottica was the site of international aid for a number of years and the old man appointed himself the official head of the Society. According to the bartender, the guy was a Brit that killed a Frenchman in Paris and was sentenced to French Guiana. Fresher made a mental note to himself that even though the man would be almost seventy five today, he could be a source of information. The story continued. After he was released, the Brit stayed and there must be money in what he is doing now or the old man wouldn't be doing what he does.

The bartender shared a few of the tales including how prisoners would escape but realized that the land was too swampy and full of snakes. No food or fresh water made jail look good. Those that didn't get swallowed up by the jungle gave up within a day on the loose. Some of them on the run would actually make it to the lava fields in the Wijck Mountains in Suriname finding precious stones or gold, and when they were caught, would use their treasure to bribe guards so that prison life wouldn't be so hard.

"You said precious stones. What kind?"

"Diamonds. Here. I got this from a prospector a few years ago. It's only a carat and rough. By the time its cut and polished, it would be less than a fifth of a carat. Not only that, but diamonds from the lava fields aren't always clear."

"Are they usually that size?"

"No. I've seen them four and five carats but again, they take a lot of work to make them saleable."

"You mentioned gold."

"There are lots of stories, but in reality, it's the natives that know where it is. They have deals with a couple of companies to mine gold, and keep the other locations secret."

"Is that one of those myths?"

"This country can create a myth about anything and anyone especially if it involves one of the better known convicts. Some of them even go beyond their antics."

The bartender went on to tell the story of a French priest sent from France to bring the word of God to small colonies in Suriname. Over time, the priest became so loved by the locals that they forged the 'Croix Pretre', a solid gold cross with polished diamonds for him to wear as a Pectoral cross. The priest went missing during one of Clousiot's escapes. There was no cross on Clousiot when he was recaptured, so the myth of the cross is that he hid it and planned to get it on his next escape.

Fresher was focussing on Kristine and the diamonds. How did she and Berger find and get the gems back to Canada?

Back in his room, Fresher created a plan, a plan that may extend more than two to three days. He would need to speak to the agency offices in Cayenne, as well as travel to Cottica then Innini and speak to the AC Society leader.

Chapter 14

By 6:30 in the morning, Fresher was towelling off after showering when the aroma of coffee drifted into his room. After he dressed and left to go downstairs, the aroma got stronger. There on the bar in the lobby was a pot of coffee and a sweet yeasty smell replaced last night's spicy curry stew.

"Good morning. Pour yourself a coffee. The buns just came out of the oven. One or two?"

"One please."

Fresher took a mug from beside the pot and poured the almost black fluid into the cup. He immediately added milk and sipped slowly. This wasn't his Sumatra blend and was certainly meant to wake a person up.

The woman from the front desk walked out of the kitchen with a plate full of buns.

"Take what you want. Breakfast is included in your room. I don't think you will need any butter."

"Thank you."

"My husband says you are heading to the relief office. They open at eight," she said before disappearing back into the kitchen.

Fresher reached for a bun and took a bite of the warm pastry. It reminded him of an éclair without the filling, delicious and light with a melt in your mouth buttery texture.

Just as he finished his bun and coffee, the two Italian back packers came down the stairs and left the hotel. Shortly after, Fresher stepped outside into a sauna. It almost took his breath away. It was only ten minutes to eight and his freshly showered body was immersed in sweat.

The Relief Agency office was at the edge of town and stood on a dirt covered street between a small general store and a car repair shop. The sign over the door read, 'South American Relief Agency for French Guiana and Suriname' in both French and English. He wasn't sure whether to knock or just walk in. Just as he got to the door, four teenagers speaking what he thought was German came out and he assumed that they were volunteers from Germany. Fresher used this as an opportunity to walk in. There were half dozen desks, each with someone at them. He went up to the closest desk and was met by a very cheerful young woman about twenty. She looked at Fresher with a big smile and asked him something in French.

He shook his head and said, "Parlez-vous Anglais?"

"Yes, I do speak English. You look a bit too old to be a volunteer. Oh, I am so sorry; I didn't mean to imply you are old." The young lady blushed."How can I help you Sir?"

"My name is Harold Fresher from Canada." He kept the Doctor title for the time being. "I am here at the request of a good friend who lost his wife recently. Her name is Kristine Locke. In her younger years she volunteered in French Guiana and I am hoping to you could help me with some information."

"Oh, I am so sorry. I'll try and do what I can. What was her name again?"

The young lady was extremely helpful. She went back to a mountain of filing cabinets for several minutes and returned with a folder. The next ten minutes was a history of Kristine and her role. Kristine Locke was a volunteer from May 1972 to June1973. She worked as a construction volunteer in Cottica which was a town on the border of French Guiana and Suriname.

'Cottica'. That was a town that the bartender mentioned last night, he recalled.

The young lady went on to tell Fresher that Kristine was on a team of twelve that included four Canadians, six Germans and two Americans. It was one of the few teams that experienced no group dynamic issues and was commended by the local government for doing such a wonderful job. Each month, the teams were given a four day pass. Most returned to Cayenne to buy some clothes, make a few phone calls back home, get a great meal and even have a cold beer. Revived, they went back to Cottica. At the end of the assignment, each volunteer received an exit interview and a free taxi ride to the airport. The assignment was for twelve months, but one of the Germans, an woman named Marta Anders plus Kristine and a volunteer named Gils Berger from Quebec City stayed for an additional two months. The agency didn't support the extra time, but did make it easy for them to find accommodations and part time work. The majority of those who extended wanted to do some site seeing sometimes going into Brazil for a few days. The governments were quite lax on volunteers as long as they still had the Agency's identification. In the case of Kristine, Berger and Anders, the Agency found a billet for them in Cormontibo which was close to Cottica. It was a larger town close to farms and the three worked as field hands. That part of the country had many crops and July and August were fruit harvesting time. Limes and sugar cane were major exports of the country and farmers could not afford to leave any product un-harvested.

"Do you have a file on Anders?"

"Give me a minute. Yes, here is her file. She was from Hanover Germany. This is interesting."

"What?"

"Well, if this is Ander's picture, she is at least fifty. We seldom get volunteers over forty."

"So, once Kristine completed her exit interview in June 1974, you never heard from her again?"

"No, there is nothing in file. Wait. Yes, there is a note from August 1973. Here, it is written in English. Read it if you want."

Fresher read the note. 'Kristine Locke and Gils Berger visited the Agency this morning on their way to the airport. They expressed their appreciation for all that the Agency did for them. Kristine lost her Agency identification card and asked if it could be replaced so that she wouldn't have any difficulty with customs on her way back to Canada. A replacement was issued.'

"Was Marta Anders with them?"

"Not according to the file"

"So where did Anders go?"

"Probably went home."

"Thank you for your kindness and information. I appreciate it. I do have one last question. What can you tell me about the Andre Clousiot Society?"

The clerk burst out laughing and went on to tell Fresher that the group was no more than a bunch of wanna-be explorers who shared some wild dreams of finding their fortune. The stories began when prisoners who were released, stayed in French Guiana to work and live because they couldn't afford transportation back to their homeland. The myths were just that - myths, like the ones a Canadian or American would hear around a camp fire after a few beers. She described the self professed leader of the AC Society as some old coot making money by telling these stories to tourists, selling them a tattoo and maps of the journeys that the prisoners took after having escaped but before getting caught. She assured Fresher it was all bogus.

****

Back at the hotel just before noon, he took another shower, put on a dry shirt and visited the bar for a cold beer.

"Can I get you a sandwich?" the co-owner bartender asked.

"No, I'm good. Just the beer."

"How did you make out at the Agency?"

"Great. I got the information I was looking for."

Fresher went on to tell the bartender about Kristine's assignment in Cottico and it was just as he thought, she was constructing of small houses in neighbouring villages.

After her year in Cottico, she had stayed on in Cormontibo and worked harvesting for a couple of months. Fresher went on to relate about how the Agency confirmed that the old man in Innini, the self professed head of the AC Society, was really an old coot who sold tattoos and maps of the journeys that the prisoners took. According to the story that went around the Agency, the old man was purported to be imprisoned at Saint -Laurent du-Maroni and after release, turned his story telling into a business.

Fresher sipped his beer then asked, "I am intrigued by the inclusion of gold and alluvial diamonds in these tales. Could there be any truth to this?"

"There sure is. I did a bit of research when I first came to this country. It turns out that alluvial diamonds is the term used to describe diamonds that have been removed from the primary source by natural erosive action over millions of years, and eventually deposited in a new environment such as a river bed, an ocean floor or a shoreline. As I suggested yesterday, there are old volcanoes in Suriname in the Wijck Mountains. These were the source of the diamonds according to stories coming out of that part of the country. The Gran Rio River is at the bottom of the mountain range, but is extremely rough terrain and very few people can get in and out without some danger, either snakes, animals, or just plain getting lost."

Fresher's mind was going a mile a minute. There were too many coincidences. Was it possible that during the two month extension, Kristine and Berger ventured into the Gran Rio River, found diamonds and smuggled them back to Canada? He needed to take his suspicion to the next level.

"What's the best way to get to Innini?

"Bus. Leaves around 9:00 every morning."

"What time does it come back?"

"Every day at 1:00."

"So I can't get there and back the same day?"

"Not if you want to stay less than an hour."

"Can you hold my room?"

"Sure. Not a lot of people waiting for the executive suite."

****

The early morning bus ride to Ininni was another true adventure. A combination of heat, dust from unpaved roads coming in through open windows, the smell of a local food brought onto the bus by the locals, and the vegetation crowding the vehicle on both sides was a memory that would never leave Fresher. Fortunately, he took the advice of the bartender and bought a back pack filled with several bottles of water. A woman sitting beside him spoke only French, but offered him a flatbread sandwich with some kind of pasty substance on it. At first, Fresher shook his head, but eventually gave into her insistence. The sandwich turned out to be quite tasty, if not a bit on the spicy side. He marvelled at how friendly all the people were and promised himself to consider French Guiana as a place to vacation in a couple of years.

Just before noon when he got off in Innini, he realized that the open bus windows provided coolness to keep his shirt dry. Now in the dead air of the street, his shirt was wet. He looked for a sign that read, 'Taverne'. His pal the bartender in Cayenne told him that it would be one of the only places in Innini to get a room for the night. The town wasn't that big. He found the clay clad single story building quite quickly and went inside. The small lobby hosted a few locals at a table in the corner drinking beer. A woman was cleaning the bar top.

"Beer please."

Without saying anything, she reached under the bar and pulled out a bottle of beer dripping cold water. She opened it and placed it in front of Fresher.

After a long drink, he put the bottle down and asked if there was a room for the night.

"No English."

Over the next few minutes and several gestures, the woman reached under the bar again and Fresher was given a key to a room in the back in exchange for five US dollars.

Fresher finished his beer and went to the room to wash up and change his shirt. The room was just that, a room. There was a window but no air conditioning and no bathroom. A second door went out back to a courtyard where there was an outhouse as well as a well with a bucket. A wash basin lay on a table nearby. He smiled inside. The only time he saw this scenario was in a western movie.

A quick wash with the cool well water, and a change to a tee shirt was followed by a seat back at the bar hoping to have some lunch. He made a hand signal as if to be putting something in his mouth. The woman at the bar smiled and brought over some flat bread and the same paste that the lady gave him on the bus. He could get used to the food, he thought.

As he was finishing his lunch, he motioned the woman over. He took his finger and outlined AC on the bar. The woman shook her head not understanding. Fresher pulled out a small notepad and pen from his pocket and wrote AC on one of the pages. The woman smiled at Fresher and took the notepad and pen from Fresher. On a clean piece of paper, she drew a street with a box with 'Taverne' written beside it. She added several boxes going to the end of the street where a smaller street ran off of it. She put three X's on that street and circled the third X.

"Merci," he said.

Fresher went back to his room and took a bottle of water. He left the hotel and proceeded to follow the map toward the end of the street. As he turned the corner, there were three hut-like structures very similar to others that he saw on his bus ride from Cayenne to Innini.

There was no sign of an AC Society.

As he approached the third hut, an older man with a long white beard and even longer hair was sitting in a chair whiling away the day under a thatched overhang on the hut. The man saw him coming from the distance and perked up. As Fresher got closer the man rose and smiled, extending a hand.

"Hello. I am John Steele. I think you are looking for me. Word travels very fast in Innini."

"I am Dr. Harold Fresher from Canada. I would be looking for you if you are connected with the AC Society." He used the doctor moniker hoping to establish credibility.

"That would be me. What can I do for you Doctor? Here to immunize the common folk. "

"No I am not a medical doctor."

"So what would you like?"

"Information."

"I charge for my time."

Fresher gave him a twenty dollar bill which Steele immediately stuffed in his pocket.

"What do you need to know?"

Fresher started by telling Steele that he was here at the request of a good friend that lost his wife recently. That was consistent with what he told others and Fresher had a sense that Steele already knew it. He went on. Her name was Kristine Locke and she was fascinated by tales and a myth to the extent that she was an active member of a university club called the Allegorists, and was particularly interested in the Andre Clousiot Society. She studied French and selected French Guiana for an international volunteer assignment after graduation. She was here from mid 1972 to August 1973. The first year she was in Cottica and then spent a couple of months in Cormontibo working as a harvester. A tattoo; 'AC' was on the back of her right shoulder which he understood was like a membership card into the Society. He also told Steele that she may have been with a young man by the name Gils Berger. Any information would be useful.

John Steele was only too happy to help, especially with twenty dollars in his pocket. He was a sixteen year old Brit looking for work in Paris when he got into a fight and killed a local. He was sentenced to twenty years at Saint-Laurent du-Maroni.

Fresher interrupted and asked him to get to Clousiot and Kristine.

Steele looked a bit indignant but continued by explaining how he met Andre Clousiot in prison. Clousiot escaped seven times, each time being recaptured until finally he was sent to Devil's Island. Clousiot's exploits were very well known among the prisoners. He was a bit of a hero. Most prisoners would never try to escape as the punishment when caught was quite severe. This didn't deter Clousiot. On one of his escapes, he was captured near the Wijck Mountains and brought back several diamonds which he used to bribe guards so that his punishment would be less severe. Fresher wasn't sure that Steele made up the story or not. Steele went on to tell of his release in 1950, however didn't have the money to return to Britain, so he meandered south to Innini and became a farm hand. Then in 1960, he happened to have met some volunteer students from North America and told a few wild tales of Clousiot. The stories went back home with the volunteers so that when a new crop of volunteers came, the tales and myths grew. It became so popular that he formed the AC Society. His prison skill of tattooing came in handy as he also tattooed those who wanted to have official membership, and sold them maps of the various escape routes that Clousiot took. Steele, having been a certified prisoner at the same time as Clousiot, was never doubted by tourists. The locals, on the other hand, laughed him off.

"I have a picture of Locke and Berger. Would you have a look for me please?"

Steele took the picture and stared at it for several seconds. "Yes, I do recall these two. She had longer hair, but that's her. There was a third person. A much older woman as I recall, not the usual myth hunters. I tattooed them all three of them. I give a special rate for two or more. Yes, I recall now. They were working in the Cottica area. Cottica is only a few miles north of here and I remember the three coming back at least four or five times looking at my route maps. I have five different route maps that are cheaper if you buy two or more."

Fresher thought, this guy is a true entrepreneur.

"Were they interested in any particular map?"

"Yes, but I was forced to stop selling that one the year before. The route went to the Grand Rio river area at the base of the Wijck Mountains. A man from Australia bought one and went off to follow the route. They found his remains three weeks later in dense jungle having been attacked by wild boars. My map was in his pocket. The officials told me that I couldn't sell that map anymore."

"So, they didn't have that map?"

Steele's face froze for a few seconds. "Well, that's not quite correct. The last time I saw the two in the picture and the older woman, they were heading back to Cayenne on their way home. I sold them the map knowing they wouldn't be going in that direction. I am sad your friend's wife died, but am somewhat relieved that they didn't take the route."

"Would you have a copy of the map?"

"Yes, I kept a few in the event that the bush was cleared someday but I am not supposed to sell them."

Fresher pulled out two more twenty dollar bills that Steele quickly took and passed him a map. He declined a tattoo for another ten dollars.

As the day was winding down, Fresher asked Steele if he wanted to join him for a beer and something to eat at the tavern. The invitation for a free beer was quickly accepted. Back at the bar, both men enjoyed a light dinner of rice and spicy chicken. Once again, Fresher was delighted with the flavouring in the simple dish.

Over dinner, Steele told Fresher a few of the tales that he crafted for tourists and students. There was Clousiot actually reaching Brazil and marrying a woman before being recaptured. The woman bore a son who is now a famous movie star. Then there was the one where Clousiot escaped to Cunani, on the coast south of Cayenne, built a raft out of coconuts and was out in the ocean for thirty three days before being rescued by a ship bound for Cayenne. He was arrested immediately and given six months in solitaire. One of the favourite stories was the escape through the swamps of the Maroni River, fighting off crocodiles, water snakes and leeches. This escape lasted only a week and Clousiot told Steele that the swamp was worse than the lashing he took for escaping. Another favourite was the coincidental disappearance of a priest named Maxille with the famous Croix Pretre when Clousiot was on one of his escapes. Fresher stared at Steele. Croix Pretre. That was the same term that the bartender in Cayenne used. Fresher listened to Steele intently as the story continued. The priest was endeared to the people in the central mountainous region of Suriname. Locals working in an abandoned mine were able to pull out a few sizeable nuggets and alluvial diamonds before they dropped to the river bank. The tale evolved to the extent that the priest was so well liked that the natives made him a gold and diamond Croix Pretre, or Cross of the Priest. Clousiot apparently found the priest on a country road, killed him and stole the cross. Steele tells the story and adds that Clousiot must have hidden the cross as he never heard of any cross after Clousiot was captured and returned to the prison. The priest's body was never found. Fresher smiled thinking that Steele should be writing novels.

"John, I have one last question. Does Matthew *7:13?*

"No, I'm not much for the bible."

"How about the numbers *21657?*"

"No, Dr. Fresher, I do not recognize them but I can see what the locals might know, for a price."

"Thanks John but I really don't think that is necessary."

The evening ended with Steele going back to his hut and Fresher crawling into a hot ruffled bed at the back of the bar. He was happy that he could leave French Guiana with more information. To him, it was clear that Kristine and Berger somehow got to the river and found some diamonds and smuggled them back to Canada. They changed names thinking that someone might come after them. There was still the mystery of the ring inscription, but that probably had no significance except that it was a reminder of the diamond issue.

****

The morning bus to Cayenne was packed, so much so that three younger travellers sat on the floor and several chicken cages had to be strapped to the roof. Fresher was down to his last two bottles of water, both warm. As he opened one, he saw one of the children staring at him. He passed the second bottle to the boy and in return received a big smile. The boy took a drink and then shared the bottle with his two friends.

Fresher walked back into the tavern and could smell today's daily special. He went to his room enjoyed a shower and reorganized for his trip back to Canada the following day.

Late afternoon, he went down to the bar and ordered a beer.

The bartender smiled. "How did you make out in Innini?"

"Good, I think. I met John Steele, the leader of the AC Society. He filled in a few blanks which will be helpful. He's quite the character, with a lot of tall tales. He did tell the whole fable about the Pretre Croix you mentioned. Must have been some cross, the way he tells the story."

"Do you want to see a picture of it?"

"You have a picture of the cross?"

The bartender went over to a pile of old magazines stacked in the corner and sifted through them. He smiled, and pulled an issue of a history magazine, opened it up, and there was a picture of Pretre Maxille with a dazzling pectoral cross that looked to be about five inches high. The craftsmanship of the cross and the polished diamonds were exquisite. The magazine was published in 1974 but the picture was taken in 1936 by a geologist. The article was about the mystery of the cross with an estimated value of over $50,000 USD.

"Interesting. According to Steele, Clousiot stole the cross and hid it."

"Anything is possible."

"By the way, what are you serving for dinner?"

"Your lucky day, we have a bean and fish roti. We only get fresh fish every couple of weeks. I'll get you a serving."

As soon as the dish was in front of him, the hot sauce invaded his nostrils. Even though the taste was outstanding, he needed a glass of water to finish dinner.

The rest of the evening was spent talking everything from politics to economy with the bartender. By ten o'clock, Fresher was beat and lay on the bed enjoying the breeze coming in from the air conditioner.

The same taxi driver that picked him up at the airport was in front of the tavern by eight in the morning. As Fresher came down the stairs, the owners were waiting to say goodbye. The woman had a bag in her hand. Fresher could smell the wonderful aroma of fresh baked buttery buns. They both shook Fresher's hand and bade him a safe trip home.

With his curiosity now satisfied he left Cayenne on the regional carrier feeling like his work was completed. The flight from Cayenne to Caracas was a repeat of the flight from Caracas to Cayenne. The air in the plane was stale and hot and was a cavalcade of smells and noises, from both the passengers and their animals. The only good thing about the flight was that it was short and he had two buns for an on-board breakfast.

The layover in Caracas allowed Fresher to get one last exposure to the hot and humid weather of South America. Although he was in the area for only a few days, he was getting somewhat acclimatized. His shirt was only partially wet. As he stood outside the airport, he reflected on the exact opposite he had endured on a much earlier case in Zugspitze, from the very, very cold to the very, very hot. He smiled and went inside to board the plane back to Canada. As he checked through the gate, the attendant smiled at him and told him that he had been selected for a free upgrade. Yes, he thought.

On board, he passed on the beer and wine preferring a glass of ice water. He never realized how good ice was. The attendant soon arrived with his meal. The dish was a letdown after the wonderful flavours he experienced in South America. He put his head back, closed his eyes satisfied that he had finished his work. Sleep did not come; rather, he kept seeing Jenn Gallager's face smiling at him when they shook hands at the restaurant.

Chapter 15

Fresher arrived back in Toronto late in the evening still needing to drive to his home in Hamilton and to get organized and call Mark for a meeting, but not until a good night's sleep.

The next morning, refreshed from a night in his own bed in a cool bedroom, a long hot shower with soap, and a full breakfast, he went to his office.

"Welcome back Harold. How was South America?"

"Like you said, hot, not and hotter. "

"There a couple of messages for you."

"Thanks. I see you are wearing the buckle I brought back from Montreal."

"Yes. In my culture, a horizontal arrow is good luck. How did you know?"

"I didn't. It was just luck."

As soon as Samid left his office, he picked up the phone and dialled Mark's number.

"Hi Mark, it's Fresher."

"Hello Harold. I was wondering when I would hear from you. Are you back?"

"Yes. Do you have any time today to drop into my office?"

"Yes, but it will have to be after 3:00 as I have a visitation this morning and a pre-wedding counselling session that will take an hour or so after lunch."

"Thanks Mark. I'll make sure Samid knows you're coming. We'll enjoy a good cup of coffee."

At 2:45, Mark arrived.

"How was French Guiana?"

"Hot and humid during the day; hot and humid during the night. Mark, you won't believe the food. I have never tasted anything so fresh and flavourful. They like their spice and heat, but in that climate, it goes very well. I even ate a flatbread sandwich with some type of spread that a woman gave me on a rural bus. It was delicious."

"Glad you enjoyed."

"That's not what I wanted to tell you."

Fresher laid out his findings from French Guiana. He didn't repeat what Mark already knew, but did tell him that Kristine and Berger were definitely volunteers in French Guiana and Suriname. They worked in a town called Cottico which was near the Wijck Mountains, and old volcanic region. They became members, so to speak, of the AC Society and had the tattoos put on by a man named John Steele. He explained who Steele was and how he became the self professed leader of the Society. Steele made a business out of tattooing and selling maps to anyone who would buy one. There was an array of various routes that Clousiot supposedly took and Steele sold as maps, however, one map he was not permitted to sell. It was a map through a very dangerous part of the jungle to where it was suspected that diamonds could be found. In fact, the authorities stepped in and stopped that sale of that particular map after a tourist purchased the map and was found dead in the jungle. Kristine and Berger convinced Steele to sell them one anyway misleading Steele by making him think they were on their way back to Canada. What he didn't know is that they extended their stay for around two months which would have given them the time to follow the map, especially since they worked as harvesters on the border of French Guiana and Suriname. No one could verify that the two ever followed the route, but Fresher was convinced that they must have as they sold raw diamonds in Montreal. He was also sure that they changed names thinking that someone might come after them. The last thing he verified was that Steele didn't know anything about the inscription on the ring.

"Mark, there was one other thing. A third person from Hanover Germany, Marta Anders was with them when they bought the map. This Anders person was not with them when they were actually on their way to the airport. I know this because the Agency has very good records."

"Who is Marta Anders?"

"According to the Agency, she was a volunteer, and from what I understand was in her fifties, quite a bit older than the traditional volunteer."

"Where is she?"

"No one knows. My guess is she got her share of the diamonds and went home."

"Thanks Harold. I think that we probably have all the answers we are going to get. There is still the mystery of the inscription, but it's not something that I think we need to chase."

"I think you're right Mark. Look, for what it's worth, Kristine made some bad choices but she buried all of that and found you. I know you will never forget the secrets she kept, but she loved you and that's really what is important."

"Thank you Harold."

As Mark reached out to shake Fresher's hand he said, "Harold, I am off to Regina next week for my parent's 40th anniversary and I thought I would talk to both my parents and Kristine's mother. I am not so sure they need to know the whole story, but if the entire Montreal story ever got to them, they would be devastated, especially Kristine's mother. I would like to give them some comfort that Kristine's life was a good life. In the end, she made a conscious decision to live a very respectable life. I also want to fess up to Mrs. Locke about you not being an insurance investigator. She needs to know that you were helping me."

"Mark, your sense of righteousness is exactly what this world needs."

"Thanks Harold. Listen, would you like you to come with me? You need a break and we can craft the story on our journey."

****

On the plane to Regina, Fresher entertained Mark with a few of the tales that Steele had told him over a few beers the day before he left French Guiana. Included was the story about a priest that was so well liked that the natives made him a gold and diamond Croix Pretre, or Cross of the Priest. As the myth goes, on one of Clousiot's escapes, he killed the priest and stole the cross. The priest's body was never found. Mark joked that it would be nice if his parishioners were that generous.

"Mark, you introduced me to Jenn Gallager in the restaurant before I went to French Guiana and I was."

Before he could finish, Mark laughed and said, "I knew that there was a connection between you two that night. What do you want to know?"

"Well, she is attractive and I didn't see any wedding ring."

"Jenn is the salt of the earth type. She is a nurse at the hospital and an integral part of the women's group at Mountaincrest. She has been divorced for about ten years. It happened long before I came to Hamilton and from what I heard she caught her husband sleeping with another woman. Fortunately, there were no children involved, and before you ask, no, there is no man in her life."

"Thanks Mark." Fresher sat back making a mental note to talk to her the next time he was at Church.

Winter had arrived in Regina and it was in stark contrast to French Guiana. In less than two weeks, Fresher went from a tee shirt and shorts to flannel shirt, sweater and wool topcoat. The taxi heater was on full blast and the two men sat in the back not wanting to remove their gloves. The sides of the roads were piled with snow and people at bus stops exhaled steamy breath. Mark already told his parents that he would be staying at the Marriot when he was in Regina. The house would be full with Mark's aunt and two uncles plus spouses staying there and he didn't feel like being relegated to the basement. His sister's house was out of the question; four children were enough to cope with. Besides, he was bringing a friend from Hamilton. In reality, this would give Fresher and himself more time to make sure the story was right.

About two miles out of town the taxi drove by one of the oldest cemeteries in the area. It was the kind of cemetery that was started by settlers and grew to house several thousand departed souls. The cemetery was surrounded by a steel fence erected in the early nineteenth century. Over the years, the road had been widened and the plowed snow was pushing up against the fence.

"Mark, I didn't see and entrance to that cemetery. How do people get in to visit?"

"It's on the other side. The original country road is still there and it's accessible from the next cross road. When I was a kid, that country road was busy. Actually, there is a very ornate entrance to Levi's Gate."

"Levi's Gate?"

"Yes Harold. That's the name of the .... Driver, take the next right and then the road behind the cemetery."

"Mark, what is going on?"

"Driver, pull over. Harold, look at the name of the cemetery."

"Yes. It says Levi's Gate, just like you said."

"Harold, Matthew also known as Levi. Matthew 7:1. *Enter by the narrow gate. For the gate is wide and the way is easy that leads to destruction, and those who enter by it are many.*"

"Harold, do you think - the inscription on the ring - could it be?"

"Would Kristine and Berger taken this same route from the airport when they went to Mr. Lock's funeral?"

"Absolutely."

"Mark, it's getting dark. Let me give this some thought. You have a big day tomorrow. We can see if there is any connection to Levi's Gate."

After the two men checked into the hotel, Mark headed to his sister's to ensure that all the arrangements for the anniversary were in place. Fresher went to the hotel restaurant and enjoyed a western Canadian steak then went for a brisk walk replaying the taxi ride and the connection between the cemetery and the inscription on the ring. On his way back to his room, he left a message for Mark through the switchboard.

'I've got some work to do in the morning. I'll be back in time to share a taxi to the party.'

Fresher ate a room service breakfast waiting for eight thirty when the City offices opened. It was a hunch, and something that caused a few sleepless hours the night before.

The clerk in archives was one of those people that loved her job and didn't hold anything back. She went through great lengths to tell Fresher that Regina meant Queen and the Queen's territory was the name used for a large part of Saskatchewan. As the communities grew, and the open range became farms and the fence became visible everywhere, including cemeteries. In the case of Levi's Gate, an ornate steel fence was erected in 1909. He clerk went on that the cemetery can hold up to six thousand and is designed with three hundred rows, with two hundred grave sites per row. The first row is just inside the narrow gate on a service road. The clerk started into a history of the older graves and Fresher politely moved the discussion back to the layout of the plots.

"Are the rows marked?"

"No. As I said, row one is the first one inside the gate and the first grave in the row is at the west end. So if you were looking for Garth Coy, I would give you row 158, grave 93. You would count 158 rows in and the 93rd grave from the west end."

Fresher left the building and headed back to the hotel excited to speak to Mark. At 1:30, Mark and another man came into the lobby.

"Harold, this is my brother in law, Russ. Can you two wait a minute? I forgot my parent's gift in my room."

The three men drove to the party not giving Harold any chance to speak with Mark. Once at in the Hiott's home, the noise level was incredible. Mark immediately found Mrs. Locke arrived and took her aside and explained who Harold really was. She hugged Mark and told him that she was happy that he wanted to bring full closure to her life.

The anniversary party was a success. Mark's sister Janet did a great job organizing the affair and the large group included many of Regina's society given that Mark's father and Russ were well known lawyers in town. Dr. Fresher was a hit as well. Most had never met a professional investigator with such credentials. Before leaving the party, Mark asked his parents and Mrs. Locke to meet Fresher and himself for breakfast at the Marriot the next morning.

Russ drove the two men back to the hotel and as soon as they were in the lobby together, Harold motioned Mark to the coffee shop.

"Mark, I may have figured out the ring mystery. You must be exhausted after today. Let's get a good night's sleep and enjoy breakfast, then I will explain."

"No Harold. Please let me in on what you have."

"It has everything to do with the cemetery we stopped at today. Look, it's late. Let's go into the details tomorrow."

"Probably a good idea, besides my mind is on telling everyone about some of Kristine's past. They need to know."

At breakfast with his parents, Mrs. Locke and Fresher, Mark took the lead and told the story of Kristine in Montreal. He excluded the murder of Berger and explained the name changes by fabricating a story that when Kristine and Berger left French Guiana, they hadn't paid a hotel bill and thought that someone may come after them. Fresher acknowledged the story. Mrs. Locke and Mark's parents were relieved that Kristine eventually saw the error of her ways and went to Mark for love and life. Inwardly, Mark thought that one small fib would be okay in order to protect Kristine's reputation. The rest of the story they knew and were happy that Kristine left the world a married and fulfilled woman.

As soon as the parents left, Mark immediately turned to Fresher who told Mark that they needed to go to the cemetery. On the way in the taxi, Harold explained the layout and numbering system of the graves. He spoke to the city yesterday and found out that there are three hundred rows with two hundred grave sites per row. Row one is at this narrow gate. Based on the number 21657, there was only one choice, row 216, grave 57. No other combination would work.

Mark knew that Fresher was on to something. The taxi dropped them off at Levi's Gate. The graveyard was massive with some of the older tombstones leaning. Many of the stones were soft granite and had suffered erosion over the years while some were moss covered and were too hard to read. The newer marble stones were intermingled with older stones, a few having flowers recently placed. Both men were in awe by the sheer size of the cemetery, especially since they didn't know what they were looking for.

Fresher and Mark walked to row 216. Mark stood there while Harold went to the west side and counted 57 graves. It was an old style stone, the type with a well weathered picture of a man near the top. It was in black and white and featured him in a high collared shirt with a tie. The picture was covered by a round piece of glass, around eight inches in diameter, milky from years of heat, cold and water. The picture frame was inset into a chiselled out depression in the stone. The inscription on the stone read, 'Peter Harris 1837-1910.'

Both men stood looking at the stone wondering what significance was. They stood there for several minutes asking each other questions. Did they know anyone named Harris? Are the years significant? Could Kristine have known Harris? Was he somehow the answer to the inscription?

Fresher noticed it first. The picture of the deceased was not as vertical as it should be. It was turned slightly to the right. Fresher leaned forward for a closer look. The frame was tampered with as he could see small pry marks under the edge of the frame. He reached in his pocket and pulled out a small folding knife. Slowly and carefully, he pried the frame away from the depression in the stone.

Fresher and Mark froze. There behind the picture was a gold and diamond cross.

It was larger than Fresher thought it would be. Just as the picture in the magazine, the gold cross was very finely crafted. The diamonds were not cut, but were polished. The centre diamond was the size of Mark's nail on his small finger. They both continued to stare at it for several minutes.

"Mark, I'm positive. This is the cross that Pretre Maxille wore when he went missing. I saw his picture wearing this cross in a magazine in Cayenne."

"Isn't that the priest you told me about on the plane?"

"Yes, and, this is the cross I saw in the picture." Fresher repeated himself three times.

Back at the hotel, they ordered dinner to Fresher's room. The cross was not going to be out of their sight.

"Harold, I feel numb. How could Kristine have been involved with this?"

"Mark, it is beginning to make more sense to me now. Kristine and Berger weren't concerned about the diamonds, they were afraid that someone would come after them for the cross. How they got it, I don't know but strongly feel that they may have found it when they followed the map that Steele gave them. Kristine and Berger knew that the diamond money was running out and no one was coming after them, so they hid it in the cemetery probably hoping to return in the near future and deal with it. That is why Berger came with Kristine to Regina. They needed to do this together. I suspect that the ring was engraved here in Regina, a roadmap so to speak, and they would decide what to do with the cross later."

"But how would they plan something so elaborately as hiding it here?"

"Harold, the majority of the Locke family is in this graveyard. Surely she knew the numbering system."

"Yes Mark, and once Berger's foray into drugs and his death, it released Kristine from the Montreal life. She wanted no part of the cross. Kristine probably thought best to leave sleeping dogs lie."

Chapter 16

The two men sat in Mark's hotel room staring at the cross.

"How do we handle this Harold?"

Fresher's mind was racing since they found the cross. He knew that the right thing to do was to return it to Suriname, but the question was how. If this wasn't handled properly, it could be very serious for the international aid volunteers, especially Canadians. There were probably a few smuggled diamonds over recent years, but the cross was a whole other matter.

"Mark, do you agree that the cross must go back?"

"Yes, Harold, and not because it belongs to the Church in Suriname, but it is a representation of Christianity and must not become the property of a collector."

The flight back to Hamilton was a quiet. Both men knew that they possessed an important part of the history of a country.

Mark took the cross and secured it in the Church's safe in the office with a plan to meet the next morning in Fresher's office. When Mark arrived, Fresher was looking over his copy of the map that Steele sold him. According to Steele, it was the same map that Kristine and Berger purchased, and the same that was now not being sold because of the danger on the route.

"Mark, if Kristine and Berger did follow this map, it must have taken them to both the diamonds and the cross. If the myth is true, Clousiot killed the priest and then hid the cross. Something doesn't make sense. Could it have been that easy for the cross to be found by two amateur explorers?"

"Harold, whatever happened, we need to find a way to return the cross as well as the map and let the Suriname authorities take it from there."

"Mark, where are those photos I gave you?"

"At home, why?"

"They may be another part of the answer."

The car ride to the Suriname Consulate in Toronto was quiet. They decided to leave the cross, the map and the photos in Hamilton.

At the Consulate, there was only a desk and a receptionist in the lobby. Mark wore his collar and Fresher flashed his credentials identifying him as a doctor. They were directed to sit in a small anteroom off to the side. No one else seemed to be waiting to see the Consulate Director. This made sense to Fresher because the Suriname Consulate probably received very few visitors and only two people were lined up in the Visa line.

Within five minutes, a woman appeared and asked them to follow her. In a large very ornate Board room, they waited only a few minutes before a man and a woman came in. The man introduced himself as the Consulate Director and the woman as is Assistant.

Fresher and Mark introduced themselves and Fresher passed his business card across the table. The Consulate Director looked at the card and looked impressed.

The meeting began very cordial. Fresher and Mark asked a few benign questions about the people of Suriname, the climate, the exports and the languages spoken there. Carefully, Fresher introduced the subject of all the myths and tales from that part of the world. The Consulate Director laughed and agreed that there were many great fables that only manifest over the generations. Fresher moved a bit more into the issue by asking about the myth of the Pretre Croix. Immediately, the mood in the room tensed. He told the Consulate Director that he read about it in a magazine while he was in French Guiana earlier in the year. The Consulate Director nervously smiled. He responded that he also read the same article and expressed his sadness that the priest disappeared. Fresher went one step further and asked if the cross was ever found. The Consulate Director stared at him and slowly shook his head. It was now time.

"Sir, we may have information that could lead you to where the cross is."

The Consulate Director's froze and he stared at Fresher. He pulled his hands together on the table and turned his head slightly and stared at Mark then back to Fresher. There was a long silence in the room.

"Reverend Hiott and Dr. Fresher, is this a joke?"

"No sir, it isn't. We are here to determine the best course of action. If we did know the location of the cross, we want to make sure that the story behind its discovery is not known by anyone except the people in this room. The cross would be returned and Suriname would release a story that it was found in the jungle by some local creoles."

"Reverend Hiott and Dr. Fresher, are you looking for a reward?"

"No. We just want what we asked for."

The following morning in Mark's office, Fresher and Mark met with the Consulate Director and the Consulate lawyer. Fresher brought with him a prepared a document exonerating Fresher and Mark. It was notarized by the lawyer.

Once signed, the cross was placed on the table in front Consulate Director and the Consulate lawyer. They stared at it for over a minute, eyes wide and mouths agape. Slowly, the Consulate Director reached out and took the cross in his hand. His fingers caressed it gently and Mark saw a tear in his eye. He looked up at Mark and Fresher without words but a look of a child thanking his Mother for an unexpected gift.

Fresher handed him the map.

"Sir, what is the map?"

"Let's just say that it may be a clue to the priest that went missing, and perhaps where the cross was found. You may also want these."

"Photographs?"

"Yes. They could help. They are numbered one through twelve and may have been used to record the actual route."

After the Consulate Director and the Consulate lawyer left, Mark sat with a blank look on his face.

"Mark, are you okay?"

"Harold, when I first learned that Kristine's past was questionable, I never in my wildest imagination thought that it would culminate here. On one hand, I feel satisfied that you uncovered the entire story. On the other, how could I be so blind? Kristine drops unto my life after years apart. I should have been more diligent."

"Mark, no doubt there were some things in her past that would make a good novel. But we resolved them. There are not many people that can reunite with a true love and spend years, albeit short, married and in love."

"Yes, you are right. I was blessed having Kristine, and particularly thankful for meeting you. Thank you."

"You're welcome. By the way, I'll invoice you by the end of the month."

"See you in Church Sunday?"

"Only if there are no more mysteries."

The two men shook hands.

Chapter 17

Two weeks before Christmas 1988, Samid brought the paper into Fresher's office. The story was very small. It spoke of a long lost priest's cross that went missing in Suriname in 1936 and it was found by Creole workers cleaning brush from a roadway. The article was no more than sixty words.

At the same time, Mark had just finished reading the article and sitting back in his leather chair, he reflected on the past year. He lost Kristine and there would always be emptiness inside him. He was, however, very happy that she made a change in her life, found him and developed into the perfect Minister's wife. He marvelled at how Harold Fresher was able to connect the clues. Sure, there was the cross issue, but Fresher handled that very well and in the end, Mark was satisfied that they did the right thing. He also decided that there was no value in telling Mrs. Locke or his family the diamonds and cross story. The memory of Kristine would remain as, a loving daughter with a husband, that she lived a life that she could live, should live and wanted to live.

The first Sunday in January 1989, Mark was in his office putting the final touch on his sermon for that morning. It was that time of year when a Minister has gone through another Christmas period. The services, the celebrations, the visiting, and the food kept Ministers busy for most days plus a few evenings. He was looking forward to a week off later in the month. Today, he was preaching on recovery. How appropriate; recovery in life, recovery after a hectic season, and recovery of things that needed to be recovered.

After the service and the obligatory shaking of hands, Mark joined the people having coffee on the lower level. He immediately spotted Fresher standing beside Jenn Gallager both obviously enjoying the conversation.

"Hello Jenn, Harold. The coffee is excellent this morning. Not as good as your blend Harold, but tasty."

Jenn Gallager excused herself and went off to the kitchen to begin to help cleanup.

"Harold, is something brewing between you and Jenn?"

"Let's just say we're both interested."

I didn't see you at the Christmas service."

"No Mark, I went back to Ottawa for Christmas with the family. It was good to see them. I got back early this week."

"I would imagine that you are having a bit of down time after last year's work."

"Actually, I have just started another case that promises to be, let me say, different.'

"Well, if you need a reference, just call."

They both laughed.

"Mark, I should tell you that I got a call from Consulate Director on Friday. He told me that the Suriname authorities sent a squad of troops into the jungle to follow the map and the photos. They discovered the remains of the priest. There wasn't much left after so many years, but enough to know it was him based on his shoes and his hat. He was at the base of a steep cliff in dense bush. The cause of death could not be determined but it was assumed that he slipped and fell. He also told me that they found an older white woman about three miles on the way back. There wasn't much left of her but her backpack had the name Marta Anders on it and there were six diamonds inside. From what they could determine she died of exposure, probably got lost.

"So that also wraps up the Marat Anders mystery as well."

"Yes Mark. Everything seems to have been answered. The Consulate Director repeated his appreciation for what we did and that the cross getting to Canada will always be a mystery. He even quipped that maybe an international aid worker came upon the body and took the cross. I told him that could be the start to a great myth."

16520866R00084

Made in the USA
Middletown, DE
23 November 2018